T0128811

What's Next?

A Path for Your New Walk With Christ

James W. Ptak

WESTBOW
PRESS
A DIVISION OF THOMAS NELSON

WestBow Press books may be ordered through booksellers or by contacting:

WestBow Press
A Division of Thomas Nelson
1663 Liberty Drive
Bloomington, IN 47403
www.westbowpress.com
1 (866) 928-1240

ISBN: 978-1-4908-1091-1 (sc)
ISBN: 978-1-4908-1092-8 (e)

Library of Congress Control Number: 2013918436

Printed in the United States of America.

WestBow Press rev. date: 10/18/2013

Table of Contents

Dedication

To my wife Carol who has encouraged me in life, love and the writing of this book, and to the Lord Jesus Christ who has given me a new life in Him through the cross. To Him be the glory.

Introduction

So God worked in your heart and you accepted Jesus as your Lord and Savior. What's next? You have lived your life according to the world and now there's something different; the world seems different, your friends seem different, and you want to learn everything you can about this wonderful God who called you to be His own. You may have accepted Jesus apart from a church, and that's great, but you need to be part of a fellowship of believers to grow and help you on this new path.

The Lord called me late in life to be His son, and later a pastor. I grew up attending church every week without having a clue as to what it meant to be a Christian. By the time I was in my early forties, God got a hold of me and made me His. But I ran into a little problem; I still had no clue. I was blessed to find a church and a couple of mentors that helped me learn, but they were a well-studied lay man and a pastor. They began by using words that I did not understand, and frankly was a bit embarrassed to ask. Words like justification and sanctification and a bunch of other words that made no sense. Well, I went back to school, attended seminary and learned all these big words and ideas that seasoned Christian's role off their tongues as if they were discussing the weather or the latest football game.

That is the reason why I wrote this book; for those who God is working on their heart, and those who God has called only recently. This is not a "systematic theology" book, but a guide to what the basics of Christianity using biblical concepts and common words to explain the doctrines of the Church. This is also not a "Christianity for Dummies" book because I find that offensive. God has made you in His image and called you to be His, so you cannot be a dummy; you are blessed, but like everyone new to something there is a steep learning curve. The Bible and the concepts about who God is do not pop into your head when you accept Jesus as your Lord and Savior, and Christianity is not a religion for the mindless. God puts into our hearts a hunger to learn about Him and His Word.

In Part 1, we will look first at the Bible; how it is divided up, how we got the books that we have, and why this book is the final authority on faith, doctrine and conduct. When I first became a Christian, I couldn't tell my Old Testament from my New Testament and why there were two; how was it written, and, can we trust it. I think this is the biggest obstacle in a new Christian's life; they see a book that is comprised of sixty-six books with various literary styles, and the first thing that we are told is to read it, and then memorize some of the verses! If you're lucky, someone will guide you as to where to start, but most of us are left on our own. Without a guide you can get discouraged and give up, missing out on the wonders of who God is and the plan that He has for you through His Word!

In Part 2, *Who is God* follows. That may seem like a huge undertaking to understand who He is but God gives us everything we need to know about Him in His Word, the Bible. We will also see who His Son Jesus is, and the meaning of His sacrifice. The Holy Spirit, the third person in this Triune God will be examined; the fruit of the Spirit and the gifts that He gives.

On the other side of the holiness of God is the *Nature of Man*. Because of the Fall of Adam we have inherited a sinful nature. Man is unable, without the help of God, to not sin. It's not in our nature, so we have to examine first what the Fall was all about and the consequences of that Fall. Then what actually is sin? Is it a deliberate act, an act of omission, or just falling short of the glory of God? The good news is that God has a plan for our salvation through Jesus. This plan called the order of salvation contains all those doctrines that we are hit with before we can understand a need for them.

Part three looks at *Death*, and the life after, the *Church*, and the *End Times*; all of which have more questions than answers, but we will try to break down these concepts using Scripture. Much has been written recently about Hell, its reality and severity, as well as the misconceptions about Heaven, with much of the misconception brought about by Medieval literature and old wives' tales. (Hint: we will not be all playing harps!) The Church has been around since Jesus ascended into Heaven, and has not changed its basic job description in two thousand years; preaching, teaching, praying and caring. But all good things come to an end with Jesus returning for His bride (the Church). The end times theme has become part of Christian literature and movies but has also confused more people than not. Pre-Trib, Post-Trib, Rapture, and Millennium will be defined and explained.

At the end of each chapter there are study questions which will help you to better understand the concepts of that chapter, such as, "What are the Dead Sea Scrolls?" "What are the gifts of the Holy Spirit?" or "What are the Sacraments of the Church?" These are questions that have concrete definitive answers but also included are questions that will make you think about the material, maybe force you to search your Bible, and ask yourself what it means to *you.*

Finally, in the last chapter there are the basic *Creeds and Confessions of the Christian Church.* These historical documents were put into place to combat the heresies that were, and are plaguing the Church. At the end of each chapter there will be a short discussion of the heresies that these Creeds and Confessions addressed. Each doctrine of God, Jesus, Man, the Bible, and others have at one time or another been attacked by non-biblical thoughts.

This book can be used as a self-tutorial, but the best way is to have someone to walk with you through this material. They can answer the immediate questions that come up and be a blessing to you and believe it or not, when you ask someone to help you, you become a blessing to them. There is nothing that a "seasoned" Christian enjoys more than to share the excitement that they have for Christ and His Church.

Unless otherwise noted, all Biblical references are from the New American Standard Bible: 1995 Update (LaHabra, CA: The Lockman Foundation, 1995).

May God bless you on this journey of *What's Next.*

Part I

The Bible

CHAPTER 1

Why Start Here?

All Scripture is inspired by God and profitable for teaching, for reproof, for correction, for training in righteousness; so that the man of God may be adequate, equipped for every good work. 2 Timothy 3:16-17 [1]

Why start with the Bible? Isn't this where all the confusion to new Christians and seekers lie? Well, we need to start with the Bible because all else stands or falls on what is written in this book; our knowledge of who God is, His love for us and His plan for our salvation is recorded in every book of the Bible. We cannot truly know God apart from His revelation to us within the pages of this book. God has given us everything we need to know, and everything that is expected of us through this method of God teaching us. But the truth is that unless God enables you to internalize

---

[1]   *New American Standard Bible: 1995 Update* (LaHabra, CA: The Lockman Foundation, 1995), 2 Ti 3:16–17.

His Word, then it becomes nothing more than literature that can be read, examined, dissected, parsed, analyzed and then forgotten. We will discuss this particular piece of the puzzle in Part II when we discuss who God is and the work of the Holy Spirit. But once we do read with the aid of the Holy Spirit;

> The words printed on the pages of my Bible give witness to the living and active revelation of the God of creation and salvation, the God of love who became the Word made flesh in Jesus, and I had better not forget it. [2]

As we look at the different doctrines I will use Bible verses to prove a statement. The format for quoting Scripture is Book Chapter: Verse (ex. John 3:16; the book of John, the third chapter, sixteenth verse).

You probably noticed already that I use interchangeably three words: the Bible, Scripture and God's Word. The word Bible comes from the Greek word *biblios*, which means "book" or the pulp from the papyrus plant that was written on in ancient times. The phrase "Word of God" or "God's Word" comes from the fact that God spoke these

---

[2] Peterson, Eugene H. *Eat This Book*, William B. Eerdmans's Publishing Company, Grand Rapids: 2006

words through the Holy Spirit to the writers of the books. Scripture just means "writings."

Why Should We Trust It?

Richard Dawkins, a noted atheist wrote:

> I think that the Bible as literature should be a compulsory part of the national curriculum—you can't understand English literature and culture without it. But insofar as theology studies the nature of the divine, it will earn the right to be taken seriously when it provides the slightest, smallest smidgen of a reason for believing in the existence of the divine. Meanwhile, we should devote as much time to studying serious theology as we devote to studying serious fairies and serious unicorns.[3]

Dawkins obviously does not trust the Bible to inform us of who God is, nor does he believe that there is a God at all. So this brings up the question "Why should we trust the Bible?" Why should rational, intelligent people believe what is written on the pages of this book and why it is

---

[3]   Dawkins, Richard. *The Independent*, 12/23/1998. http://richard dawkins.net/quotes/52 (10/12/2011)

believed to be the bestselling book in history with some estimates upwards of six billion copies being sold? Are we being fooled by a book that has no more relevance than a Charles Dickens novel? Some would argue that Dickens is more relevant, but Christians worldwide put their faith in what they believe to be God-inspired writings. What makes us trust it? How do we know what is written is true?

Self-attesting—We say that Scripture is self-attesting, meaning that it speaks for itself. It says it is God's Word, so it is God's Word. Confused? There has to be an ultimate source of knowledge, one that teaches us all we need to know about ourselves and about God. This may seem like a circular argument, but we all argue in this way to prove our point. An empiricist, one who believes that all we know can only come from our senses argues that we there is nothing outside our senses because they believe so. They come with the idea that there is nothing outside the sense so when they do not find anything outside their senses it reinforces their philosophy.

The Bible tells us that it is the Word of God. In the King James Version of the Bible (we will get into different versions later) the phrase "Thus saith the Lord" appears 415 times in the Old Testament. It does not say "thus saith Moses" or "thus saith Joshua" but "thus saith the LORD" attesting to that it was God who spoke these words to the prophets and writers. This had special meaning in ancient Israel because if a prophet would say this phrase it was true, and to disobey the prophet who said this would be to disobey God himself. In the book of Exodus that relates the Israelites flight from Egypt, Moses approaches Pharaoh of Egypt and asks him to release the Israelites from slavery.

> And the Lord spake unto Moses, Go unto Pharaoh, and say unto him, Thus saith the Lord, Let my people go, that they may serve me. [2] And if thou refuse to let *them* go, behold, I will smite all thy borders with frogs. Exodus 8:1-2 (KJV)

Since we all saw Charlton Heston in the movie *The Ten Commandments*, we know that Pharaoh did not obey and so frogs invaded Egypt. God spoke through Moses, commanded something with the promise of punishment for not obeying, Pharaoh does not comply, and God is true to His Word. So when we see "Thus saith the Lord" or a modern translation Like the New International Version's "This is what the Lord says," God is speaking through His prophets as if He were speaking directly to us.

In the New Testament we have the words of Jesus. Seventy-six times does Jesus say *"Truly I tell you"* indicating that what He was about to say is as we would say now, the Gospel truth. Jesus used this phrase whenever He wanted to impart some authenticity to His statements. For example Jesus, in speaking about John the Baptist says *"Truly I say to you, among those born of women there has not arisen anyone greater than John the Baptist! Yet the one who is least in the kingdom of heaven is greater than he."* Matthew 11:8 (NASB). Jesus making a twofold point where He is commending John, but at the same time prophesying about the kingdom of heaven. But they are the words of Jesus, accurately recorded in the Gospels giving credence to the text.

Historically accurate—Unlike other "sacred texts" the Bible is historically accurate. Archeology has uncovered evidence of the kings of Israel, cities that were mentioned in the Old Testament that are no longer known by that name, ancient civilizations, and events that once were thought to be the fantasies of the biblical authors. Evidence since has confirmed events including wars, exiles to foreign countries and even the flood. This story, thought by some to be one of sheer imagination a counterpart in other historical documents;

> A Sumerian king list from c. 2100 BC divides itself into two categories: those kings who ruled before a great flood and those who ruled after it. One of the earliest examples of Sumero-Akkadian-Babylonian literature, the Gilgamesh Epic, describes a

great flood sent as punishment by the gods, with humanity saved only when the pious Utnapishtim (AKA, "the Mesopotamian Noah") builds a ship and saves the animal world thereon.[4]

Each year new evidence is revealed supporting the Bible rather than disproving it; a plaque in Caesarea with the name of Pontius Pilate, or an ossuary (bone box) of the high priest Caiaphas. Revelations regarding both Old Testament and New Testament times are being uncovered almost daily. Publications such as *Biblical Archaeology Review* and *Bible and Spade* offer the latest in archaeological research results that a layman can understand.

Another area in which we can see the historical accuracy of the Bible is in the documents that have been found in recent times. Beginning in 1947 with the discovery of the Dead Sea Scrolls which are a series of 972 documents that date to between the 2nd and 1st centuries BC, either full scrolls containing Old Testament books or fragments thereof. These scrolls are consistent with the content of our present Bible. These scrolls are some of the Old Testament books, of which the Isaiah Scroll is the most

---

[4]   Maier, Paul L. Biblical Archeology: Factual Evidence to Support the Historicity of the Bible. *Christian Research Journal*, vol 27 no 2. (2004)

complete, and scrolls that are historical glimpses into the community of the Essenes who hid the scrolls.

Internally consistent—What does it mean to be internally consistent, and why is that important? Scripture never contradicts itself. We can look from Genesis to Revelation and observe a consistent, constant message. The words of Jesus do not contradict the words of the prophets; the words of Paul do not contradict the words of the Torah (the first five books of the Old Testament), and none of the psalmists contradict the historical books of the Old Testament. Each book reinforces the message written by the other writers. Peter in his second letter wrote about Paul and his writings:

> ...and regard the patience of our Lord *as* salvation; just as also our beloved brother Paul, according to the wisdom given him, wrote to you, as also in all *his* letters, speaking in them of these things, in which are some things hard to understand, which the untaught and unstable distort, as *they do* also the rest of the Scriptures, to their own destruction. 2 Peter 3:15-16

Peter was affirming the writings of Paul as being of the same caliber and importance as the rest of Scripture.

So the Bible is internally consistent, historically accurate and self-attesting, but this book that we hold in such high regard is more. If it was just these then it would be a great book of information. The purpose of the Bible is not for pure informative purposes but for formative purposes. The words are to transform the reader to know God and what God's will is for them. If we read the Bible for information, we may as well be reading Shakespeare or Milton. The Bible has that power. God's Word, according to the prophet Isaiah wrote:

> *so is my word that goes out from my mouth: It will not return to me empty, but will accomplish what I desire and achieve the purpose for which I sent it.* Isaiah 55:11

Inerrancy—Get a group of biblical scholars in a room and ask them to define inerrancy and you will get as many answers as people in the room. Some define it as "indefectibility" others as "infallibility," and yet others as "indeceivability." This term of inerrancy is tossed around like a Frisbee on a sunny beach with about as much care. R. Laird Harris wrote in his book, *Exploring the Basics of the Bible*:

> The Bible is verbally inspired, it is infallible, and it is inerrant in the manuscripts as they were originally written. The statement of

faith of the Evangelical Theological Society expresses it briefly but well: "The Bible alone, and the Bible in its entirety, is the Word of God written and is therefore inerrant in the autographs [original documents]."[5]

Notice the last three words of this statement: "in the autographs." We do not have the autographs, we have copies. God in His wisdom did not allow the original writings to survive lest we begin worshipping the book rather than the One who inspired the book. But does that means that the book is flawed because of centuries of copyists and translations and interpretations? Absolutely not! We can with certainty affirm that the Bible, according to the Lausanne Covenant is "without error in all that it affirms." It is inerrant in all that it teaches. 2 Timothy 3:16-17 *All Scripture is inspired by God and profitable for teaching, for reproof, for correction, for training in righteousness; so that the man of God may be adequate, equipped for every good work.* [6]

Clarity—Here's a word that you can use next time you play Scrabble: perspicuity. This pretentious word has a simple meaning; the Bible is sufficiently clear by itself for

---

[5] R. Laird Harris, *Exploring the Basics of the Bible* (Wheaton, Ill.: Crossway Books, 2002), 10.

[6] *NewAmerican Standard Bible: 1995 Update* (LaHabra, CA: The Lockman Foundation, 1995), 2 Ti 3:16–17.

believers to understand. You can pick up a Bible, read it and understand what God is telling you without having a seminary degree, a shelf full of books, or an interpreter to tell you what God has made plain. Now all these other things are useful especially a good teacher that will help you develop good interpretive habits. Using concordances, dictionaries and commentaries helps in understanding the context of the passage, but the meaning of the passage is usually pretty clear by itself.

Sufficiency—Wayne Grudem defines sufficiency as: "The sufficiency of Scripture means that Scripture contained all the words that God intended His people to have at each stage of redemptive history, and that it now contains everything we need God to tell us for salvation, for trusting Him perfectly, and for obeying Him perfectly."[7] Let's unpack this a bit. During each stage in human history, God provided His Word, for exactly that time. The Bible was written over a two thousand year period by different men for different reasons according to the inspiration of the Holy Spirit; the Torah (first five books) to give Israel the Law, the history books to remind them of their past and what God had done for them, the Wisdom books to lead them on a better path and the Prophets when they forgot the first three sections. Then Jesus comes and now the

---

[7]   Grudem, Wayne. *Biblical Doctrine: Essential Teachings of the Christian Faith* (Grand rapids: Zondervan Publishing House, 1999), 58.

Gentiles (non-Jews) are invited into the plan of salvation that was once for the Jew only. So we have the Gospels and the Letters, leading us to Christ. Each stage we are given everything we need to know God and to trust and obey Him.

What has happened almost since the time of the Apostles is that there were, and continue to be, some people who believe that Scripture is not enough. It began in the second century with the "other gospels" written by heretics called the Gnostics. They thought that there was more that we had to learn and wrote these fraudulent gospels under the name of actual Apostles. We have the Gospel of Thomas, the Gospel of Judas and the Gospel of Barnabas, all of which were written after the Apostles died. Other than the obvious error in authorship, we see that these do not meet the criteria for inclusion in the Bible; they are not consistent with the rest of Scripture. Today we have the *Book of Mormon* written by Joseph Smith in the nineteenth century and *Science and Health with a Key to Scripture* by Mary Baker Eddy of the Christian Science religion.

<u>What's Next?</u>

Next we will explore the Bible for its contents and talk a bit about translations. As we said in the sufficiency of Scripture, remember that the Bible was written at different times in history but relevant to today's world. Each word that was God-breathed has relevance to you, right now.

Study Questions:

1. Look up in a dictionary the words inerrant and infallible. Use these words in describing Scripture.
2. What does "self-attesting" mean? Why is this important?
3. What is "perspicuity"?

Meditative Questions:

1. Look up 2 Timothy 3:16-17. How does this verse fit with your ideas about the Bible?
2. Does the fact that there are no autographs in existence bothersome to you? Why or why not?
3. Look at other religions "sacred texts." Do they fulfill the criteria of being self-attesting, historically accurate and internally consistent? Are they consistent with the Bible?

CHAPTER 2

The Book of Books

I testify to everyone who hears the words of the prophecy of this book: if anyone adds to them, God will add to him the plagues which are written in this book; and if anyone takes away from the words of the book of this prophecy, God will take away his part from the tree of life and from the holy city, which are written in this book. Rev 22:18-18 [8]

The Bible is a book of books, sixty-six in all written from the time of Moses (c. 15th century B.C.) to the Book of Revelation (c. 95 A.D.). Three different languages, different authors and different periods in history can make reading the Bible a challenge, now add translations to the mix and it gets down right confusing. Let's look at this sacred book of Christianity and try to sort some of this out.

---

[8] *New American Standard Bible : 1995 Update* (LaHabra, CA: The Lockman Foundation, 1995), Re 22:18-19.

Languages

The Bible was written in three languages: Hebrew, Aramaic and Greek. The Old Testament was written primarily in Hebrew but there were some that were written in Aramaic. Aramaic is an ancient language that is still used in some parts of the Middle East and can be traced to the beginnings of both the Hebrew and Arabic languages. This was the common language of Israel after the exile, and was probably the language that Jesus spoke.

The New Testament was written in Greek. As we study these New Testament writings we can see two distinct forms of Greek: *koine*, which was the form that the everyman spoke, and a classical Greek used by the scholars of the time.

This seems very simple; Old Testament in Hebrew and New Testament I Greek, except there is a Greek Old Testament. This is called the Septuagint, sometimes written as LXX.

It derives its name from the popular notion that seventy-two translators were employed on it by the direction of Ptolemy Philadelphus, king of Egypt, and that it was accomplished in seventy-two days, for the use of the Jews residing in that country. There is no historical warrant for this notion.[9]

This translation was written about the 3rd century B.C. and to add to our confusion contains more books than some of our present day Bibles. The LXX contains seven additional books not contained in the Hebrew Bible. The process began in the 3rd century B.C. when Jews were dispersed throughout the world where the common language was Greek. The Scriptures were translated, but since there was no official canon, these extra books were placed with the ones we have. The Hebrew Bible canon was formally adopted at the Council of Jamnia in 70 A.D when the LXX's contents were not canonized and these extra books were removed. But Jerome in the 4th century translated the LXX into Latin, to become known as the Latin Vulgate and reinserted the disputed books, becoming the official Bible of the Church. It wasn't until Martin Luther began his translation that he went back to the Hebrew Scriptures without the extra books, and that's how the Protestant Bible came into being. These extra books, AKA Deuterocononical Books are useful for reading, as some give a history that is not contained in the others, and wisdom in the writings of Sirach and Baruch can be applicable as other wisdom books in the Bible.

---

[9]   M.G. Easton, *Easton's Bible Dictionary* (Oak Harbor, WA: Logos Research Systems, Inc., 1996).

Translations

So let's decide on English as the language we will study. A quick scan of Christian Books.com lists twenty-seven versions of the Bible in English. What's the best and what's the best for you, and what is the difference? Translations fall into three categories: word for word translations, thought for thought translations and paraphrases. Here are the three categories and a translation of Romans 3:25

Word for Word—This is also known as formal equivalence and is as close to a word for word translation that we can get. There are some liberties because if it were an exact word for word translation the reading of it would be so difficult as to make it useless. These Bible translations seem a bit woody in the flow of reading; not as you would speak, but they offer some of the best scholarship and accuracy in translation. Versions that would fall into this category that are still popular today would be the *King James Version*, the *New American Standard*, and the *New Revised Standard* bibles.

The King James Version has been with us since 1611 and has become the standard by which all other Bibles are measured. Some churches will not use anything else, and is considered to the THE Bible version and no others are allowed. This misses out on some easier to understand translations as this version is still in the old English with the Thees and the Thous. But reading the Psalms in the version is so poetic it almost seems wrong to read them in any other version.

The New American Standard is also a good version. Below is Romans 3:25 in each of the types of translations.

> NASB—whom God displayed publicly as a propitiation in His blood through faith. *This was* to demonstrate His righteousness, because in the forbearance of God He passed over the sins previously committed;[10]

Thought for Thought—Also known as dynamic equivalence, these Bibles are easier to read but sometimes words are used that really do not convey the original meaning of the sentence. The most popular version in this category is the *New International Version.* Others include the *New American Bible*, the *New English Translation* and the *Holman Christian Standard Bible.*

> NIV—God presented him as a sacrifice of atonement, through faith in his blood. He did this to demonstrate his justice, because

---

[10] *New American Standard Bible : 1995 Update* (LaHabra, CA: The Lockman Foundation, 1995), Ro 3:25.

in his forbearance he had left the sins
committed beforehand unpunished—[11]

Paraphrase—These Bibles take the basic story and put it into the authors own words. Eugene Peterson's *The Message* is the most used in this genre and is a wonderful way to get the Bible story for the meaning.

The Message—God sacrificed Jesus on the altar of the world to clear that world of sin. Having faith in him sets us in the clear. God decided on this course of action in full view of the public—to set the world in the clear with himself through the sacrifice of Jesus, finally taking care of the sins he had so patiently endured.[12]

All three are saying the same thing only in different words and levels of difficulty. I continue to use all three depending on the need for which I am reading. When preparing a message for Sunday morning I read all three to get the idea of the passage, and then I rely on the NASB for the scholarship of that version. In my personal devotional

[11] *The Holy Bible: New International Version*, electronic ed. (Grand Rapids, MI: Zondervan, 1996), Ro 3:25.

[12] Eugene H. Peterson, *The Message : The Bible in Contemporary Language* (Colorado Springs, Colo.: NavPress, 2002), Ro 3:25.

reading I like the NIV, but there is no wrong choice. The only wrong choice is not reading the Bible.

The Book

The Old Testament

The Old Testament is divided into four areas and thirty-nine books: the Law, History; Wisdom; Prophets. Given to Israel at different times, this is what Jesus studied, this is what Jesus quoted and this is what the writers of the New Testament knew and quoted in their writings. As young Jewish boys were made to study the Law and if they proved to be adept at their studies they would go on to the rest of the Scriptures under the tutelage of a rabbi.

The Law—These first five books of the Bible, Genesis, Exodus, Leviticus, Numbers and Deuteronomy are also known as the Torah and the Pentateuch. Even if you have never read the Bible, you probably have a cursory knowledge of the stories in Genesis. Here you find the creation story, of how God created the heavens and the earth and everything in it; Adam and Eve in the Garden and their Fall from grace, Noah and the flood, the patriarchs (Abraham, Isaac and Jacob) and the story of Joseph (made into a Broadway musical).

The second book of the law is Exodus; the story of the plight of the Hebrew nation in Egypt and how they fled there for a land promised them by God. Moses leads the nation and their travels take forty years (would have been less if they listened to God) an God gives Israel the Ten Commandments and instruction on building the Tabernacle, which was to be the dwelling place of God as they wandered the dessert.

Leviticus is the worship book. In it contains the rules for worshipping God through sacrifice, purity and priesthood. The Jewish festivals are outlined and the dietary laws are proscribed.

Numbers begins with a census of the Israelites in the desert as God prepares them for conflict with the nations that they will encounter, but there is dissention among the people and for their lack of trust in God, no one from that generation would see the promised land, so they wander for forty years until the next generation enters the land.

Deuteronomy closes out the Torah and similar to Leviticus gives many laws and rule by which to live. Where Leviticus dealt primarily with laws concerning the relationship with God, Deuteronomy is more about the laws concerning the layman. In this book you will also find an abbreviated Ten Commandments. This is Moses' last words before he dies just short of entering the Promised Land.

History—The books in this section are just what it sounds like; the history of Israel from the time that they take over the Promised Land to through the period of kings, the exile and the return from exile. Notable stories in this section are David and Goliath, David and Bathsheba, Solomon's wise judgment, and all the kings that ruled the divided kingdom. These books are: Joshua, Judges, Ruth, 1 & 2 Samuel, 1 & 2 Kings, 1 & 2 Chronicles, Ezra, Nehemiah and Esther. These books span a period of about one thousand years from c. 1405-473 B.C. Joshua, Judges and Ruth are called the Theocratic books because God was ruler over Israel. Samuel, Kings and Chronicles are the Monarchial books as Israel was led by kings, and Ezra, Nehemiah and Esther are Restoration books, when Israel returns from exile.

Wisdom—These are the poetical books of the Bible; they were written as poems. This section begins with Job. We all know the phrase "he has the patience of Job" but what does that really mean. This book explores the plight of poor Job and his argument with God. (God wins the argument) The Psalms follow; one hundred and fifty psalms divided into five "Books" exploring every human experience and feeling. There are psalms of praise, psalms of complaint; even psalm of war, any emotion that you have felt is reflected in these psalms. These Psalms were written over a period of almost one thousand years with Psalm 90 by Moses, a majority by David (about a third), the Sons of Korah and some by Asaph.

Solomon gives us the next three books; Proverbs, Ecclesiastes, and Song of Solomon. Proverbs was written as a guide for parents to raise their children, Ecclesiastes is Solomon reflecting on his life, and Song of Solomon is a love story between a man and a woman.

Prophets—This last section of the Old Testament is the writings of the prophets that God had chosen to be His voice. There are four Major Prophets (Isaiah, Jeremiah (with Lamentations), Ezekiel and Daniel. Then there are the Minor Prophets (Hosea-Malachi). These are not the AA team versus the major leagues, but the prophets are just as important only they wrote less. It is in this part of the Old Testament that we find many of the prophecies about the coming Messiah many of which were quoted by the Gospel writers.

The Prophets can be divided up into three categories: pre-exilic (before the exile), exilic (during the exile) and post-exilic (after the exile).

Prophet	Time Period	Audience	Years of Ministry
Isaiah	Pre-Exile	Judah	740-680
Jeremiah	Pre-Exile	Judah	627-580
Ezekiel	Exile	Exiles in Babylon	593-571
Daniel	Exile	Exiles in Babylon	605-535
Hosea	Pre-Exile	Israel	755-715
Joel	Pre-Exile	Judah	835
Amos	Pre-Exile	Israel	760-753
Obadiah	Pre-Exile	Edom	848-841
Jonah	Pre-Exile	Assyria	782-753
Micah	Pre-Exile	Judah	735-700
Nahum	Pre-Exile	Assyria	664-654
Habakkuk	Pre-Exile	Judah	609-605
Zephaniah	Pre-Exile	Judah	632-628
Haggai	Post-Exile	Jews who returned to Jerusalem from Babylon	520
Zechariah	Post-Exile	Jews who returned to Jerusalem from Babylon	520-480
Malachi	Post-Exile	Jews who returned to Jerusalem from Babylon	432-424

The New Testament

The books of the New Testament begin with the birth of Jesus and end with Jesus returning victoriously to defeat Satan. These books can be divided into: Gospels, Acts, Paul's letters to the churches, Pastoral letters by James, Peter and John, Hebrews and Revelation.

Gospels—There are four Gospels in the Bible. Do not listen to the cable TV station that claims there are more than these four. There are only four, and have been since John wrote his as the last of the series. The other "gospels" were written a century or two after the apostles had died. These are part of a group of writings that were found in Egypt known as the Nag Hamadi scrolls, and were part of a heretical cult in the late second to early third century called the Gnostics. They do not meet the criteria for inclusion in the Bible as they are not internally consistent with the other writings. These are fun to read but of no spiritual value.

The four Gospels are by Matthew, the tax collector who became and Apostle, Mark, who was not an Apostle, but was closely associated with Peter and recorded his remembrances, Luke, the physician, also not an Apostle but an associate of Paul and a researcher, and lastly John, the Apostle that Jesus loved (his words). Each Gospel brings out a different view for a different audience of Jesus.

First let's start with a definition of what a Gospel is: The Greek word *euaggelion* is translated gospel. This word means "good news" or "glad tidings." The English word gospel comes from the old Anglo-Saxon "godspell" which means "God's story" or "good story." So a Gospel is a "good news" story about the life and ministry of Jesus. There are two "types" of Gospels; first are the synoptic Gospels. These are the ones written by Matthew, Mark and Luke and are called synoptic because they come from a similar perspective. Synoptic in Greek means "with one eye" so when we read these three we see that there are many similarities; the same stories, the same events and the same people. Then we turn to the Gospel of John. There is a different feel to the Gospel; John's focus is that, as he writes in John 20:31

> but these have been written so that you may believe that Jesus is the Christ, the Son of God; and that believing you may have life in His name. [13]

John's Gospel is a wonderful place to begin your Bible reading. It has some familiar stories, but more importantly we get the best picture of who Jesus is. John uses a technique called dualism where he contrasts good and

---

[13] *New American Standard Bible : 1995 Update* (LaHabra, CA: The Lockman Foundation, 1995), Jn 20:31.

evil with light and darkness. Read the prolog of John's Gospel to get a good picture of this. The Prolog is the first eighteen verse of chapter one.

Matthew and Luke give us the birth narrative of Jesus, and the genealogy of Jesus, and Luke tells us about John the Baptist's birth. Mark begins his Gospel with Jesus' baptism by John the Baptist. In Luke's Gospel there are eleven parables not found in other gospels including the parable of the Prodigal Son. Each Gospel has a different emphasis to it: Matthew is about Jesus as Messiah/King whose main audience was the Jews; Mark's emphasis was Jesus as Son of God; Luke emphasized Jesus' humanity and compassion, and John as stated earlier was that Jesus was the Christ, the Son of God.

In the synoptic Gospels you will find the use of parable by Jesus. A parable is a usually short fictitious story that illustrates a moral attitude or a religious principle.[14] The Catholic Encyclopedia states:

> There are no parables in St. John's Gospel. In the Synoptics Mark has only one peculiar to himself, the seed growing secretly (4:26); he has three which are common to Matthew

---

[14] Inc Merriam-Webster, *Merriam-Webster's Collegiate Dictionary.*, 10th ed. (Springfield, Mass., U.S.A.: Merriam-Webster, 1996).

and Luke: the sower, mustard seed, and wicked husbandman. Two more are found in the same Gospels, the leaven and the lost sheep. Of the rest, eighteen belong to the third and ten to the first Evangelist. Thus we reckon thirty-three in all; but some have raised the number even to sixty, by including proverbial expressions.[15]

Acts—written by Luke, Acts is a history of the Church in the first thirty years. The story of Acts (AKA Acts of the Apostles) begins at the Assumption of Jesus into heaven giving the Apostles a commission that would be the outline for the Book. This is found in Acts 1:8 "and you shall be My witnesses both in Jerusalem, and in all Judea and Samaria, and even to the remotest part of the earth." [16] It begins with the Apostles preaching in Jerusalem and then with the conversion of Paul, spread throughout the world. Acts is an historical account and it gives us the basis for understanding the letters that Paul wrote to the various churches and the people that are mentioned in them. The story ends with Paul imprisoned in Rome awaiting an audience with Caesar, yet still preaching the good news.

---

[15] _. The Catholic Encyclopedia. New Advent.org. http://www.newadvent.org/cathen/11460a.htm. (accessed 11-2-11)

[16] *New American Standard Bible : 1995 Update* (LaHabra, CA: The Lockman Foundation, 1995), Ac 1:8.

The Pauline Letters—Paul is the most prolific of the New Testament writers accounting for thirteen of the twenty-seven books. These letters to the various churches address issues that the churches were facing after Paul had left them, and to two of his protégés who he left to lead the church in Ephesus (Timothy) and Crete (Titus). Paul also wrote a personal letter to Philemon to let a former slave return without any repercussions. Romans is probably the most theological, but it is in Ephesians where we find that statement of salvation in Ephesians 2:8-9 *For by grace you have been saved through faith; and that not of yourselves, it is the gift of God; not as a result of works, so that no one may boast.* [17] We will discuss this more in length in another chapter.

Hebrews—This letter to the Hebrews is by an unknown author, those many speculate that it was written by Paul though Martin Luther believed that Apollos wrote it based on Acts 18:24-26. The early Church father, Tertullian in about 225 A.D. thought that the Apostle Barnabas wrote it based on Acts 4:36-37. There is no authoritative statement on the authorship of this letter, but that doesn't stop a good debate. This letter has two main themes; the supremacy of Christ, as the author writes that He is superior to angels (1:5-2:18) and to Moses (3:1-4:13). The second theme is

---

[17] *New American Standard Bible : 1995 Update* (LaHabra, CA: The Lockman Foundation, 1995), Eph 2:8–9.

Jesus as High Priest. The Jews understood the need for a priest and Jesus fulfilled the duties of High Priest as no human priest could.

Chapter eleven is the chapter on faith beginning with a clear definition of faith. Hebrews 11:1 *Now faith is the assurance of things hoped for, the conviction of things not seen.* [18]

Pastoral Letters—these are the letters written by James, Peter, John and Jude. The letters are in most cases non-specific in audience, but reveal these men as true pastors to the churches. James emphasizes the ethical life of a Christian and that faith without works is dead. Martin Luther wanted to eliminate this letter for the canon because of this statement. He rightly understood that we are saved by grace not by what we do, but this letter emphasized that we need to do something to demonstrate our faith.

Peter's two letters are a source of encouragement for those undergoing persecution, while John's letters address the right behavior and attitude of Christians. Jude warns the readers about false teachers.

---

[18] *New American Standard Bible : 1995 Update* (LaHabra, CA: The Lockman Foundation, 1995), Heb 11:1.

Revelation—The title of this book comes from *Apokalypsis* (Greek word meaning that which is being uncovered) and is the prophetic book about the ends times. The author of this book is John the Apostle, and is the one book that has more interpretations than any other. Some look at this book as all the prophecy has been fulfilled, these people are called Preterists. Then there are those who believe only some of the prophecies have already occurred, these are partial preterists, and then we have those who believe that all the prophecies have yet to be fulfilled.

Interrelation—When you first begin to read the Scriptures and go between the Old and the New Testaments, you will find much in common. The writers of the New Testament quote the Old Testament regularly and depending on the audience. As we saw above, the Letter to the Hebrews was written to a Jewish audience and is filled with Old Testament quotations and to ideas that were given in the Torah. When we read Revelation we notice the amazing imagery that is also found in the books of Daniel and Ezekiel. Luke tells us about two of Jesus' disciples walking down the road to Emmaus. They encounter the risen Jesus (though He hid his identity from them) and as they were talking:

> Then beginning with Moses and with all the
> prophets, He explained to them the things

concerning Himself in all the Scriptures. [19]

(Luke 24:27)

Jesus fulfilled the prophecies of the Old Testament, and explained this to these two disciples.

The Bible is not a novel that we read and put away, we re-read for a twofold purpose: to know God and to know what He expects of us; knowing God and His works and creation, knowing God for His love and mercy, and knowing God as He has revealed Himself to us. We are also to be transformed by the Word; our lives cannot be the same when we know what God expects from us; we have to live according to His commands and bear the fruit of our salvation.

<u>What's Next</u>

Now that we have a better understanding of the Bible we can mine from these sacred words a knowledge of who God is, His attributes, and His Creation.

---

[19] *New American Standard Bible : 1995 Update* (LaHabra, CA: The Lockman Foundation, 1995), Lk 24:27.

Study Questions:

1. Name the five books of the Law.
2. Where would we find the story of the Flood?
3. Where is the story of David and Goliath?
4. How many Psalms are there?
5. Name the four "major prophets."
6. Name the four Gospels in order.
7. Name the letters that were NOT written by Paul.

Meditation Questions:

1. Read Deuteronomy 6:6-7. What is this saying about the importance of Scripture?
2. In John's Gospel there are seven "I am" statements by Jesus. Find these seven and meditate on what Jesus is telling you about Himself.

Part 2

Who is God

CHAPTER 3

God

"I am the L*ORD* *your God, who brought you out of the land of Egypt, out of the house of slavery. "You shall have no other gods before Me". Exodus 20:2-3* [20]

Who is God? This is a question that has been on the minds of man since creation. Adam knew God personally until he was removed from Eden because of his sin, but we are not so fortunate to meet God face to face and talk with Him or walk with Him as Enoch did (Genesis 5:22). We have to get to know God through His Word and His creation. First, we are His creation, and in His creation, God put, as John Calvin the sixteenth century Swiss Reformer wrote in his *The Institutes of the Christian Religion*, that God had put a "seed of religion" in each one of us.

---

[20]   *New American Standard Bible : 1995 Update* (LaHabra, CA: The Lockman Foundation, 1995), Ex 20:2–3.

had the minds of men not been previously imbued with that uniform belief in God, from which, as from its seed, the religious propensity springs. [21]

What that means is that each one of us knows that there is a God, but in the darkness of our sin, we cannot see, and refuse to acknowledge something greater than our minds can imagine. Paul writes about this in Romans 1:20-21

For since the creation of the world His invisible attributes, His eternal power and divine nature, have been clearly seen, being understood through what has been made, so that they are without excuse. For even though they knew God, they did not honor Him as God or give thanks, but they became futile in their speculations, and their foolish heart was darkened. [22]

In the news we are hearing much about atheists who are trying to deny the existence of God, and belittle anyone who holds such a belief. So we need to really have a definition of what an atheist is and what an agnostic

---

[21] John Calvin, *Institutes of the Christian Religion* (Bellingham, WA: Logos Research Systems, Inc., 1997).

[22] *New American Standard Bible : 1995 Update* (LaHabra, CA: The Lockman Foundation, 1995), Ro 1:20–21.

is. First the atheist; if we break down the word we get a-theist. A "theist" is one who believes in God, and when you put an "a" in front of a word it become a "no." This word atheist comes from the Greek "a-theos" meaning no God. So in contemporary understanding, an atheist says there is no God (see Psalm 14:1). Richard Dawkins who I quoted in Chapter 1 is an extreme example of an atheist. His mission in life seems to be to rid the world of this "primitive" idea that a God exists.

Being an agnostic maybe is where you are right now; just not sure. An agnostic says that there is not enough information to say definitively is there is or there is not a God. You may be struggling with this; you have this "feeling" that there is a God, yet you see the state of the world, the sin and the evil that exists; the suffering, hunger and war, and you say to yourself that there cannot be a loving God and still all these problems. We will talk about this more later. For now continue reading His Word and He will make His presence known to you.

Before you think that this is a recent development, that denying the existence of God is something that came out of the Enlightenment Period of philosophy, David wrote in Psalm 14:1 *"The fool has said in his heart, "There is no God.""* Man has been denying the existence of God since man was removed from Eden, but God gives us many ways in which we can recognize Him, and know Him; sort of. We can never truly understand God to the fullest. If we did, we would be gods ourselves since God is great, perfect and righteous that we cannot understand Him. Psalm 145:3 says that His greatness is unsearchable, Psalm 147:5 tells us that His understanding is beyond measure and Paul wrote in Romans 11:33 that His judgments are unsearchable and His ways unfathomable.

If God is so far above us, His ways unfathomable, can we really know Him? God gave us everything we need to know about Him and His plan for us in the Scriptures. (see why that's where we started?) By being in His Word regularly we mine new nuggets of information about Him as he releases them through His Holy Spirit. It is in the continuous reading of the Bible that we get to know God better. It's like listening to a symphony; you cannot hear everything on the first hearing, but after numerous times you begin to pick out the flute part against the rest of the orchestra, or how the violins are chasing the woodwinds. Each time we listen, we hear something new; and that is in a finite piece of music, imagine how much we can learn about an infinite God by continual reading of His Word to us? We learn far more than facts about God when we read, we get to know Him personally. That is because the Hoy Spirit enables us to know God and not just facts about God.

The "omnis"

God makes Himself know through His attributes, the major three are His omnipresence, omnipotence and omniscience. These three give us a better understanding of what and who God is.

Omnipresence—Wayne Grudem defines omnipresence as: "God does not have size or spatial dimensions, and is present at every point of space with His whole being, yet God acts differently in different places."[23] The psalmist David wrote about God's omnipresence in Psalm 139. Eugene Peterson paraphrased psalm 139:7-12 as:

> Is there any place I can go to avoid your
>   Spirit?
> to be out of your sight?
> If I climb to the sky, you're there!
> If I go underground, you're there!
> If I flew on morning's wings
> to the far western horizon,
> You'd find me in a minute—
> you're already there waiting!
> Then I said to myself, "Oh, he even sees me
>   in the dark!
> At night I'm immersed in the light!"

---

[23] Grudem. p. 78

> It's a fact: darkness isn't dark to you;
> night and day, darkness and light, they're all
> the same to you.[24]

This Psalm tells us a couple of things; first, God is everywhere at all times. He rhetorically asks Jeremiah "Do I not fill the heavens and the earth?" (Jeremiah 23:24b) It is not just part of God at different places the totality of God in every place. The second item we get from this Psalm is that God does not have spatial dimensions. He is not made of stone or wood that man could fashion, a God that cannot be limited by our concepts of space and time, but beyond our imaginings. Solomon (David's son), when he was dedicating the Temple that he had built for God asks "Behold, heaven and the highest heaven cannot contain You, how much less this house which I have built!" [25] Solomon, famous for his wisdom understood that the Temple that he had constructed for God could not contain Him, not matter how elaborate, how fancy, or how much gold was used to make it. God was in the temple in the same way that He is in the universe, or your own heart. God's ability to be in all places and all things allows us to realize the closeness that we have to this God who loves us.

---

[24]   Eugene H. Peterson, *The Message : The Bible in Contemporary Language* (Colorado Springs, Colo.: NavPress, 2002), Ps 139:7–12.

[25]   *New American Standard Bible : 1995 Update* (LaHabra, CA: The Lockman Foundation, 1995), 1 Ki 8:27.

<u>Omnipotence</u>—Basically put, God has all the power. He has created all things, and by His power sustains all things. Galileo regarding God's power and the vastness of it wrote "The sun, with all those planets revolving around it and dependent upon it, can still ripen a bunch of grapes as if it had nothing else in the universe to do." [26] There are many examples of God's power throughout the Bible; the parting of the Red Sea, the stopping of the sun's movement (actually the earth's movement), and the flood itself shows how the earth and sky and everything in it obeys and is controlled by Him. The author of Hebrews wrote that God "upholds all things by the word of His power" and when the men told Abraham that Sarah was going to have a baby in her advanced years, they asked the rhetorical question "Is anything too difficult for the Lord?" Jeremiah 32:27 "Behold, I am the Lord, the God of all flesh; is anything too difficult for Me?"[27] cf. Mt 19:26; Eph 3:20.

<u>Omniscience</u>—God has perfect knowledge of all things that are, have been or will be. In Job 37:16, one of Job's friends says that God is "perfect in knowledge" He knows all the physical creation. Psalm 147:4 He counts the number

---

[26] Paul Lee Tan, *Encyclopedia of 7700 Illustrations: Signs of the Times* (Garland, TX: Bible Communications, Inc., 1996).

[27] *New American Standard Bible : 1995 Update* (LaHabra, CA: The Lockman Foundation, 1995), Je 32:27.

of the stars; He gives names to all of them. [28] He knows every creature; Matthew 10:29 "Are not two sparrows sold for a cent? And *yet* not one of them will fall to the ground apart from your Father." [29] and He knows each man's heart. Psalm 33:15 "He who fashions the hearts of them all, He who understands all their works."[30] Again from Psalm 139, David addresses God's omniscience and the knowing of man's heart.

O Lord, You have searched me and known *me*.
You know when I sit down and when I rise up;
You understand my thought from afar.
You scrutinize my path and my lying down,
And are intimately acquainted with all my ways.
Even before there is a word on my tongue,
Behold, O Lord, You know it all.
You have enclosed me behind and before,
And laid Your hand upon me.
Such knowledge is too wonderful for me;
It is *too* high, I cannot attain to it. [31]

---

[28] *New American Standard Bible : 1995 Update* (LaHabra, CA: The Lockman Foundation, 1995), Ps 147:4.

[29] *New American Standard Bible : 1995 Update* (LaHabra, CA: The Lockman Foundation, 1995), Mt 10:29.

[30] *New American Standard Bible : 1995 Update* (LaHabra, CA: The Lockman Foundation, 1995), Ps 33:15.

[31] *New American Standard Bible : 1995 Update* (LaHabra, CA: The Lockman Foundation, 1995), Ps 139:1–6.

Part of God's omniscience is His wisdom. God, who knows the beginning from the end and all created things, also has perfect wisdom to accomplish His perfect goals. Psalm 104:24 shows the connection of God's power, and wisdom "O Lord, how many are Your works! In wisdom You have made them all;" [32] God created all things in through His power and by His wisdom.

These three attributes of God is summed up in the classic church hymn *Immortal, Invisible, God Only Wise.*

> Immortal, invisible, God only wise,
> In light inaccessible hid from our eyes,
> Most blessed, most glorious, the Ancient
> of Days,
> Almighty, victorious, thy great Name we
> praise.
>
> Unresting, unhasting, and silent as light,
> Nor wanting, nor wasting, thou rulest in
> might;
> Thy justice like mountains high soaring
> above
> Thy clouds which are fountains of goodness
> and love.

---

[32] *New American Standard Bible : 1995 Update* (LaHabra, CA: The Lockman Foundation, 1995), Ps 104:24.

God's Moral Attributes—These are the attributes of God that we would expect from God; He is perfect in all things.

Immutability—This is the attribute that we hold on to; that God never changes; He is the same today as He was yesterday and will be tomorrow. Psalm 102:27 *"But You are the same, And Your years will not come to an end."*[33] His promises never change, His Word never changes, His love never changes... This is the hope that we have; that God promised us salvation through His Son Jesus, and all who confess Him as Lord will be saved (Romans 10:9-10), and if we confess, we will have eternal life.

Goodness—How do you measure what is "good?" The goodness of God means that everything He does and is, is the final standard for goodness. God cannot do anything that is not good. He cannot sin and He cannot do evil. The Psalm repeatedly proclaims the goodness of God. Psalm 106:1 and others begin with "Oh give thanks to the Lord, for He is good" God's goodness is manifested in many ways; mercy to those deserving of punishment, compassion for those who are suffering, grace to all people. God's common grace extends to all people; this being proved that we are still alive, and that the sun still shines and the rains come in season.

---

[33] *New American Standard Bible: 1995 Update*, (LaHabra, CA: The Lockman Foundation, 1995). Ps 102:27.

<u>Love</u>—God's love is an extension of His goodness. As with all His attributes, God does not only contain these attributes, He is the attribute. Love is a perfect example. Throughout Scripture we see God loving His people through protection, deliverance, salvation, adoption, but God according to the Apostle John in his first letter writes that "God <u>is</u> love" not that He only loves, but He is love. Paul wrote I Ephesians 2:4 "But God, being rich in mercy, because of His great love with which He loved us…" [34]

<u>Holiness</u>—We can look at God's holiness in two ways; the first is that He is perfect in every detail with no trace of stain in Him, or the second way to see His holiness is to see Him as being wholly separate from everything that is not perfect. This is the Old Testament concept and is seen when God separates something for His service; we have holy ground (Ex 3:5), or all the items that are called holy in the Tabernacle. These things were set aside, separated for use in worship to God. Israel was called a "holy nation" when God called them out of Egypt to be separated from the other civilizations. That was the purpose of circumcision and the other purity laws that were given them; to separate them from everyone else. God is His holiness is separate from us by a huge chasm

---

[34] *New American Standard Bible : 1995 Update* (LaHabra, CA: The Lockman Foundation, 1995), Eph 2:4.

called sin. Later we will see how God bridged that chasm that we now have access to Him.

Righteousness—Just as God is the final standard for goodness, He is also the final standard for righteousness or justice. God always acts justly. I know that this may seem like a false statement seeing the state of the world and what we see as injustice on God's part towards humanity, but God cannot do anything that is not just or righteous. In the Song of Moses from Deuteronomy 32:4 sang "The Rock! His work is perfect, For all His ways are just; A God of faithfulness and without injustice, Righteous and upright is He." [35] Because of God's righteousness, He punishes sin, and since Paul write in Romans 3:23 "for all have sinned and fall short of the glory of God" [36] we are deserving of punishment. But God, in His mercy and love and grace and patience does not exact His punishment on us yet, and has made a way for us to have the appearance of righteousness before Him. More on this later.

As I said before, God does not only act according to these attributes, He is the attribute; He is love, He is holy, He is righteous, and He is good. We cannot separate God's

---

[35] *New American Standard Bible : 1995 Update* (LaHabra, CA: The Lockman Foundation, 1995), Dt 32:4.

[36] *New American Standard Bible : 1995 Update* (LaHabra, CA: The Lockman Foundation, 1995), Ro 3:23.

actions from His person, as Mary sang in her Magnificat in Luke 1:49 "Holy is His name."

Worship—Now that we have established who God is we now need to examine our response to this God; that response is worship. The word "worship" comes from an old English word that means "worth-ship;" that God is worthy of our praise; the only One who is worthy. Psalm 95:6-7a says "Come, let us worship and bow down, Let us kneel before the LORD our Maker. *For He is our God.*" [37] That is why we worship; He is our God, and that is how we worship; on our knees, in humility. But worship is about so much more than the external process. John Piper wrote:

> To make it crystal clear, when I speak of worship, I do not limit what I mean to corporate events where Christians sing. That is one expression of worship. But you can sing and read the Scriptures and pray and *not* be worshipping, because worship is first and most essentially an act of the heart, It is being satisfied with all that God is for us in Jesus. That satisfaction can be expressed in song or in visiting a prisoner." [38]

[37] New American Standard Bible : 1995 Update (LaHabra, CA: The Lockman Foundation, 1995), Ps 95:6–7.

[38] Piper, John. *Desiring God: Meditations of a Christian Hedonist.* Colorado Springs, CO: Multnomah Books, 2003. 83.

<u>Glorify</u>—One of the most confusing aspect of worship is the understanding of glory and the action of glorifying. Luckily, God gives us wonderful instructions and definitions in His Word. Thomas Watson in his sermon "Man's Chief End is to Glorify God" writes that: Glorifying God consists in four things: 1. Appreciation, 2. Adoration, 3. Affection, 4. Subjection. [39] Worship is a part of our glorifying God. As will be discussed later, appreciation (thanksgiving), adoration and affection are part of our worship and part of our prayer life. Where we mainly glorify God is as Watson writes, is out of subjection. I know that is a word that seems to rub us the wrong way; we like our independence and are subject to no one. But God calls us to obedience; to obey His commandments and live according to His Word. We glorify God in the way we live our lives. If we claim Jesus as our Savior and say that it is no longer I who live but Jesus in me, then our lives MUST reflect that. If we say that Jesus is Lord, and that we as His subjects are obligated to obedience and a life that reflects that Lordship of Jesus. Romans 12:1 gives us a perspective of glorifying God: *"...to present your bodies a living and holy sacrifice, acceptable to God, which is your spiritual service of worship."* [40]

---

[39] Watson, Thomas. *Man's Chief End is to Glorify God.* puritansermons.com. Accessed 6-5-12.

[40] New American Standard Bible : 1995 Update, Ro 12:1 (LaHabra, CA: The Lockman Foundation, 1995).

Our obedience is not to be robotic or forced, for that does not glorify God, our obedience is a response to God's love and mercy for us. *"Each one must do just as he has purposed in his heart, <u>not grudgingly or under compulsion</u>, for God loves a cheerful giver."* (2 Cor 9:7) [41]

Prayer—Prayer is that communication that you have with God. As we look at the book of Psalms, we find the prayer book of the Church. In these one hundred and fifty psalms, or prayer, we find every emotion that man can face and how he can relate these emotions to God. David, the author of many of these prayers expresses his joy, sorrow, thanksgiving and even ager with/at God and his enemies. As we read these, it is almost as if we are eavesdropping on an intimate conversation; and that is what prayer is. Prayer is that conversation with your Creator. I know you are probably saying that it is a one-way conversation, but when you are truly in prayer, God will answer you; sometimes deep within your heart, and sometimes with tangible answered prayers. John Piper in his book *Desiring God* wrote that prayer is about relationship.

"...no Christian can have fullness of joy without vital fellowship with Jesus Christ.

---

[41] New American Standard Bible : 1995 Update, 2 Co 9:7 (LaHabra, CA: The Lockman Foundation, 1995).

Knowledge about Him will not do. Work for Him will not do. We must have a personal, vital fellowship with Him; otherwise, Christianity becomes a joyless burden."[42]

There are different types of prayer, and they can all be part of you daily routine (notice I said DAILY). There is an acronym to help you in how to pray; ACTS. Acts stand for Adoration, Contrition, Thanksgiving, Supplication.

Adoration—So often we use the word "adore" for many things; we adore our spouse, we adore our house (?) and women adore that little black dress (I know it's not PC), but that ONLY One who is truly worthy of our adoration is God. As we read through the Psalms we see that the writers of these prayers most often begin with statements of praise and adoration. Ps 103:1 *Bless the LORD, O my soul, And all that is within me, bless His holy name.* [43] This is only one example, and I encourage you to read through the Psalms and look at the praise and adoration that the psalmists begin with, especially the later ones.

Contrition—Contrition is being sorry for your sins, and we all commit them. So as you are talking to God in prayer

---

[42] Piper, John. *Desiring God: Meditations of a Christian Hedonist.* Colorado Springs, CO: Multnomah Books, 2003. 175.

[43] New American Standard Bible : 1995 Update (LaHabra, CA: The Lockman Foundation, 1995), Ps 103:1.

(remember it is a conversation) confess your sins, seek forgiveness and repent (turn away from them). Psalm 32:5 shows us how to confess and be contrite: *I acknowledged my sin to You, And my iniquity I did not hide; I said, "I will confess my transgressions to the LORD"; And You forgave the guilt of my sin.*[44]

Thanksgiving—We learn at an early age to say "thank you" whenever we get something or someone does something for us. When we think, truly think, about everything that God has given us (life, health, wealth, relationships…) it would be hard not to fall on our knees in thanksgiving. When we pray, it gives us a time to reflect on all that God, in His grace and mercy, has given. Paul in his letter to the Colossian Church, wrote: *"Devote yourselves to prayer, keeping alert in it with an attitude of thanksgiving."*[45]

Supplication—This is where we pour out our hearts desires to the One who can give. We pray for other's healing, salvation, jobs, family problems as well as our own wants and needs. Notice we do not begin our prayer time with this; it would be like having your father go away on a business trip and when he returns the first thing you ask him is "what did you bring me?" We do not start with

---

[44] New American Standard Bible : 1995 Update, (LaHabra, CA: The Lockman Foundation, 1995), Ps 32:5.

[45] New American Standard Bible : 1995 Update, Col 4:2 (LaHabra, CA: The Lockman Foundation, 1995).

a "laundry list" of requests, but we do make our wants and needs known to God. Let me clarify that last sentence; we do not need to let God know what we need and what we want, He already knows, but we are to go to Him, prayerfully, thankfully, verbalizing those desires. In Psalm 5, David pours out his heart, pleading for God to hear him: *Give ear to my words, O LORD, Consider my groaning. Heed the sound of my cry for help, my King and my God, For to You I pray.*[46]

The "Lord's Prayer," that prayer that Jesus taught in Matthew 6, shows us how to pray, though He does not follow the ACTS formula. He begins with Adoration, "Hallowed be your name" then Jesus moves to supplication in "give us this day our daily bread." Following this we confess and ask forgiveness in "forgive us our debts as we forgive..." ending with more praise and adoration "For Thine is the kingdom and power and glory forever. Amen"

Music—From the beginning of time, man has worship God in song. In Genesis 4:21 we are told that Jubal was the "father" of the musicians. 1 Chronicles 16:4-6 names the musicians that were to serve in the Temple, and even Jesus sang. At the Last Supper recorded in Mark 14:26 Jesus and the disciples sang a hymn as they left for

---

[46] New American Standard Bible : 1995 Update, Ps 5:1–2 (LaHabra, CA: The Lockman Foundation, 1995).

the Mount of Olives. So music and song have been an integral part of worship, but it has also been the reason for more church splits that any doctrinal issue. Music is to glorify and honor God, not to make us feel good about our worship. Music, whether classic hymns of Luther, Newton, or Watts, or new praise music of Chris Tomlin or the David Crowder Band, are meant to lead people in praise of God.

The debate that is in the Church is are we sing for or about God? Music, songs and hymns are to be both; we sing of the wondrous things that God has done as the psalms which are also songs do. They remember the Exodus event and David remembers God's faithfulness throughout his kingship. So too we sing about the wondrous things that God has done; we sing about Jesus and His sacrifice on the Cross, we sing about how our sins were taken away and how we will be with Jesus in the end. We also need to sing FOR God; this is scriptural in that we sing the same things that the heavenly host sings: "Holy, Holy, Holy." What has happened since the eighteenth century is more a focus on us rather than God. If we look at the songs from then until now, we see more songs that begin with "I" and songs about us than songs about or for God. We have to remember who we are and more importantly who God is; worthy of all our praise.

<u>The Trinity</u>

The Trinity is a unique doctrine to Christianity. While Judaism is the foundation on which Christianity is based, the concept of a Triune God does not exist in their tenets, although we see each of the three persons of the Trinity in the Old Testament Scriptures. It is this doctrine that caused part of the persecution of the Church by the Romans. They mistakenly thought that we worship many gods rather than one God, three persons. The irony of this persecution is the pantheon of gods that the Romans worshipped. Let's begin with a simple definition of the Trinity; one God, three persons; Father, Son and Holy Spirit, co-eternal, of one essence. All the attributes that were discussed above regarding God applies to each of the three persons of the Triune Godhead. The term "Trinity" does not exist anywhere in Scripture, but there are numerous examples of the concept. Paul in his letter to the Ephesian Church wrote that the whole process of our salvation is through the Triune God. Paul writes that we were "chosen in Him before the foundations of the world."(Eph 1:4); "In Him we have redemption through His blood" [47] (Eph 1:7), and "sealed in Him with the Holy Spirit of promise"[48] (Eph 1:13).

---

[47] *New American Standard Bible : 1995 Update* (LaHabra, CA: The Lockman Foundation, 1995), Eph 1:7.

[48] *New American Standard Bible : 1995 Update* (LaHabra, CA: The Lockman Foundation, 1995), Eph 1:13.

The Father—The first person of the Trinity is the Father. The idea of Father is focused on the relationship with the second person of the trinity; Jesus. In the Old Testament, God is Father of Israel (Exodus 4:22) or God of the Jews, but the idea that God is OUR Father is not an Old Testament concept; not until Jesus taught His disciples to pray by saying "our Father, who art in heaven..." was the thought that God is our Father; individually, and as a Church.

The idea of God as Father of individuals is not found in the Old Testament. Jewish thought did not turn to this concept until the 10th century AD in rabbinic writings.When Jesus prayed what we now know as the Lord's Prayer, and He prayed "Our Father" He was using the term in a way that the Jews did not immediately grasp. Paul I believe reinforces this idea when he writes about being adopted into the Father's family, becoming sons and daughters of the Father. (Romans 8:17)

The Son—Jesus is the second person of the trinity, and is the Son of the Father; co-equal and co-eternal with the Father, and as the Nicene Creed states, that Jesus was "begotten, not made, of one Being with the Father." What this saying is that Jesus is not a lesser god that was made from the one God, but that they are and always have been one. We will look at the person and work of Jesus in the next chapter.

<u>The Holy Spirit</u>—The Comforter, the Advocate, the third person of the Triune God. Again from the Nicene Creed "We believe in the Holy Spirit, the Lord, the giver of life, who proceeds from the Father and the Son. With the Father and the Son he is worshiped and glorified."

As we look at this third person of the Trinity, we find that the person of the Holy Spirit is not really defined thoroughly in the Old Testament. We get a better understanding of who He is through the authors of the New Testament and the teachings of Jesus in the Gospels. In the following pages the person of the Holy Spirit will be examined from both an Old Testament and a New Testament perspective and we will look briefly at His functions and the gifts that He gives.

The Holy Spirit is the third person of the Triune God, and as such, exhibits all the attributes of the Father and the Son, including the three "omnis;" omniscience, omnipresence, omnipotence. As part of the Trinity, the Holy Spirit was form eternity; He always existed, and was always active in both the creation and in man since Adam.

<u>The Holy Spirit in the Old Testament</u>—The person of the Holy Spirit, as stated above, is not really defined in the Old Testament. Even the name "Holy Spirit" only occurs three times (Ps 51:11; Isaiah 63:10; 11). Other names for the Holy Spirit in the Old Testament are "Spirit of God," "Spirit of the Lord," "My Spirit," and "the Spirit." The work

of the Holy Spirit is evident from the second verse of the Bible. Genesis 1:2b states, *"and the Spirit of God was moving over the surface of the waters."* [49] Louis Berkhof wrote "It is evident from the Old Testament that the origin of life, its maintenance, and development depend on the operation of the Holy Spirit."[50] Let's look at the work of the main Holy Spirit in the Old Testament.

Inspiration—the Old Testament prophets were inspired by the Holy Spirit to write the prophecies to the Israelites. Isaiah, Daniel, Ezekiel, Elijah and others relied on the Spirit of God (the Holy Spirit) to fill them with the visions, and power to speak what God calls them to. Micah give us the best description of how God works in the prophets; by the power of the Spirit Micah preached the warning to Israel during the time of their rebellion against God during a time of great social injustice. Micah3:8 *On the other hand I am filled with power—With the Spirit of the Lord—And with justice and courage To make known to Jacob his rebellious act, Even to Israel his sin.*[51]

---

[49] *New American Standard Bible : 1995 Update* (LaHabra, CA: The Lockman Foundation, 1995), Ge 1:2.

[50] Berkhof, Louis. Systematic Theology, New Combined Edition. Grand Rapids: William B. Eerdmans Publishing Company. 1996. 425.

[51] *New American Standard Bible : 1995 Update* (LaHabra, CA: The Lockman Foundation, 1995), Mic 3:8.

God did not only inspire prophets with His Spirit, but others as well. The Spirit filled the judges like Gideon (Judges 6:34), kings like David (1 Sam 16:13; 2 Sam 23:2), leaders like Moses and the seventy elders (Num 11:17; 25-29) and regular workers like you and me; craftsmen who did the work of building the Tabernacle (Ex 31:3).

The Holy Spirit in the New Testament—The person and work of the Holy Spirit is better defined in the New Testament, beginning with being called the Holy Spirit. In the Gospels the Holy Spirit is made known before Jesus is born. In Luke's Gospel, he tells us that the Holy Spirit would fill John the Baptist (1:15-17; 1:80) and His father Zechariah (1:67) and John's mother Elizabeth (1:41-42). In the life and ministry of Jesus the Holy Spirit was evident and promised. When Jesus was baptized by John, the Holy Spirit descended upon Him like a dove (Mark 1:10). Jesus promises the disciples that they too would be filled with the Holy Spirit after Jesus was to leave them. Jesus promised that when they are brought into the synagogues and questioned for their belief in Jesus, the Holy Spirit would fill them and they would know what to say (Luke 12:11-12). In John's Gospel, Jesus gives the disciples hope that when Jesus leaves them that they will be sent a Helper to aid them in their remembering all the things that Jesus taught them (John 14:15ff) and they do receive the Holy Spirit in John when Jesus appears to them after His death and resurrection in the upper room where they were gathered; Jesus breathed on them and they received the Holy Spirit.

Paul is where we get the most defined doctrine of the Holy Spirit. In his letters, Paul assumes a Triune God when he writes in 2 Corinthians 13:14 *The grace of the Lord Jesus Christ, and the love of God, and the fellowship of the Holy Spirit, be with you all.* [52] But it is Paul's writings on the fruit and the gifts of the Holy Spirit that help us in understanding the Holy Spirit. The fruit of the Spirit, as described in Galatians 5:22 are those things (love, joy, peace, patience, kindness, goodness, faithfulness, gentleness, self-control) that are the result of being filled with the Holy Spirit.

Gifts—There is no better way to get a theological argument (maybe a "spirited" debate) going is to discuss the gifts of the Holy Spirit. In Romans 12 and 1 Corinthians 12, Paul describes these gifts, some ordinary (if a gift of the Holy Spirit can be ordinary) like wisdom, mercy, faith, teaching... or they can be the charismatic gifts like healing, prophecy, tongues and miracles. There are those that defend the position that these charismatic gifts were available only to the early Church and went away after the death of the Apostles, as one of the gifts that Paul writes about is apostleship.

---

[52] *New American Standard Bible : 1995 Update* (LaHabra, CA: The Lockman Foundation, 1995), 2 Co 13:14.

Others would contend that these gifts are still extant. Those of a more traditional background are more likely to the cessation of these gifts while those for a Pentecostal background would find them normative. The charismatic movement as we know it now can be traced to the early part of the Twentieth century and the Azusa Street Revival beginning in 1906. This movement and Pentecostalism have too many branches to discuss thoroughly here, but there are branches that hold that you are not filled with the Holy Spirit unless you speak in tongues. Since Scripture is silent on the duration of these gifts, I too will be silent. One thing that Paul makes very clear is that these gifts are not given to each person (1 Cor 12:27-31) and that these gifts are for the betterment of the Church (1 Cor 12:7), if you do have the gift of tongues, then that gift is to be used in conjunction with one who has the gift of interpretation for the good of the Church; if one has the gift of prophecy then he must prophesy for the good of the Church; all gifts are for the good of the church, both "ordinary" and charismatic.

The Holy Spirit as Guide—John 16:13 *"But when He, the Spirit of truth, comes, He will guide you into all the truth; for He will not speak on His own initiative, but whatever He hears, He will speak; and He will disclose to you what is to come."* [53] The Holy Spirit is active in you; that's right, in

---

[53] *New American Standard Bible : 1995 Update* (LaHabra, CA: The Lockman Foundation, 1995), Jn 16:13.

YOU! He has been since before you confessed Jesus to be your Savior. In Chapter 7 we discuss more thoroughly the doctrine of salvation in which the Holy Spirit works from the initial call on our hearts to the final sanctification of our spirits. God promises in Ezekiel 11:19-20 that He will take our hearts of stone and give us a heart of flesh that would be receptive to His Word. Your new birth comes from the Holy Spirit. Jesus said in John 3:5-6 *"Truly, truly, I say to you, unless one is born of water and the Spirit he cannot enter into the kingdom of God. "That which is born of the flesh is flesh, and that which is born of the Spirit is spirit.* [54]

After He works to soften your heart of stone and you accept Jesus as your Savior, the Holy Spirit then works in you towards a life that is in keeping with that confession. He enables you with the "fruit of the Spirit" to lead a more holy life; this process is called sanctification, and it is a process. The Holy Spirit does not zap you and you become perfect in action and attitude (you continue to sin), but works in you that you become more and more holy, and less apt to sin. He is your Guide through this process; never leaving you on your own again; He is that voice that some would call a conscience, wanting you to live a life that God has intended.

---

[54] *New American Standard Bible : 1995 Update* (LaHabra, CA: The Lockman Foundation, 1995), Jn 3:5–6.

As a Guide, the Holy Spirit helps us pray. Romans 8:26-27 *In the same way the Spirit also helps our weakness; for we do not know how to pray as we should, but the Spirit Himself intercedes for us with groanings too deep for words; and He who searches the hearts knows what the mind of the Spirit is, because He intercedes for the saints according to the will of God.*[55] As a Guide, the Holy Spirit teaches us about God (1 Cor 2:10; 13), about Jesus (John 16:14) and about the truth (John 14:26).

The Holy Spirit guides, enables, gifts and dwells within us. This short chapter only touches on the wonder that is the Holy Spirit. We will see later how He works in the process of salvation from beginning to end. One concluding thought before we move on; you would not be reading this book unless the Holy Spirit was working in you. Without Him preparing the way, you would have no interest in God, the Bible or in God's plan for your eternal life.

Any attempt at trying to equate the Trinity with any human idea ultimately fails. People have tried to use an egg as an illustration for the Trinity, the three parts of the egg showing the three parts of the Trinity fail in that with this example, and all others, there are three individual and separable parts. An egg can be separated into the white, the yolk

---

55   *New American Standard Bible : 1995 Update* (LaHabra, CA: The Lockman Foundation, 1995), Ro 8:26–27.

and the shell, where the Trinity cannot be separated; they are One, indivisible God. There also have been many heresies regarding the Trinity which was the reason for the Nicene Council to meet in 325 AD and again in 381 AD; each heresy wrongly describing the Trinity.

Heresies Regarding the Trinity

Modalism—In this heresy, God appears to us in different forms at different times. So when Jesus was on the earth that was a manifestation of God at that time. In the Old Testament times, God appeared as Father, the Son walked the earth, and after He ascended, the Holy Spirit came to the Church. This denies that there is one God, three individual persons, at all times.

Arianism—Here the Son and the Holy Spirit are lesser gods, created by the Father. According this heresy, there was a time when the Son did not exist, nor did the Holy Spirit. This was the main heresy which the Council of Nicea fought.

Tritheism—Three gods, denying that there is but one God.

Creation—We cannot know God without knowing His creation. God has created everything from the smallest sub-atomic particle to the largest mountain, to the entire universe; all are the works of His hands. The Triune

God was at work in the creation of all things. John 1:3 "Through him all things were made; without him nothing was made that has been made."[56] This is in reference to Jesus, or as John refers to Him as the Logos (Word), is present with the Father during the creative process, and Genesis 1:2 says that the Spirit of God was present. All of created things, both inanimate and living (you and me) were created by God.

> For by Him all things were created, *both* in the heavens and on earth, visible and invisible, whether thrones or dominions or rulers or authorities—all things have been created through Him and for Him.[57] Colossians 1:6

> Who made heaven and earth, The sea and all that is in them; [58] Psalm 146:6

Scientists Dilemma—Science wants to dismiss a higher power involved in creation of the universe; they analyze data, and run simulations trying to duplicate its

---

[56] *The Holy Bible: New International Version*, electronic ed. (Grand Rapids, MI: Zondervan, 1996), Jn 1:3.

[57] *New American Standard Bible : 1995 Update* (LaHabra, CA: The Lockman Foundation, 1995), Col 1:16.

[58] *New American Standard Bible : 1995 Update* (LaHabra, CA: The Lockman Foundation, 1995), Ps 146:6.

creation, yet they are stymied by one crucial question; where did the original material come from the exploded in the "big bang" that created the universe as we know it? It reminds me of the joke about a scientist talking to God;

> God is sitting in Heaven when a scientist says to Him, "Lord, we don't need you anymore. Science has finally figured out a way to create life out of nothing. In other words, we can now do what you did in the 'beginning'."
> "Oh, is that so? Tell me..." replies God.
> "Well," says the scientist, "we can take dirt and form it into the likeness of You and breathe life into it, thus creating man."
> "Well, that's interesting. Show Me."
> So the scientist bends down to the earth and starts to mold the soil
> "Oh no, no, no..." interrupts God, "Get your own dirt."

God created all things *ex nihilo*, or from nothing. In the beginning was God, and by His Word, created all things. The creation was, and is, by His hand, for His glory, and for man to understand who God is. Let's look at some Scripture verses that define these three purposes.

By His Hand—Psalm 95:5 *"The sea is His, for it was He who made it, And His hands formed the dry land."*[59]

For His Glory—Psalm 19:1 *The heavens are telling of the glory of God; And their expanse is declaring the work of His hands.* [60]

For Man to Understand God—Romans 1:20 *For since the creation of the world His invisible attributes, His eternal power and divine nature, have been clearly seen, being understood through what has been made, so that they are without excuse.* [61]

Angels, Satan and Demons—No discussion of creation can be completed without the examining the created beings of God; those that are not man, but also not God.

Angels—Angels are the Divine Messengers of God. They are spirit, though they do take on the appearance of men as they did when appearing to Abraham (Gen 18:2), or to the Apostles at the Ascension of Jesus in Acts 1:10. They deliver messages from God for specific purposes.

---

[59] *New American Standard Bible : 1995 Update* (LaHabra, CA: The Lockman Foundation, 1995), Ps 95:5.

[60] *New American Standard Bible : 1995 Update* (LaHabra, CA: The Lockman Foundation, 1995), Ps 19:1.

[61] *New American Standard Bible : 1995 Update* (LaHabra, CA: The Lockman Foundation, 1995), Ro 1:20.

Mary was told by an angel that she would bear a son, though she was a virgin, and He would be called Jesus. (Luke 1:26-32) An angel appeared to Joseph warning him to take Mary and the new born Jesus to Egypt while Herod slaughtered all children less than two years of age, protecting Jesus from harm. But all the messages from the angels protect, God uses the angels to deliver the judgments of God. When Jerusalem was under siege by the Assyrians, God sent His angel to aid the Jews. 2 Kings 19:35 tells us, "Then it happened that night that the angel of the Lord went out and struck 185,000 in the camp of the Assyrians"[62] We do not know how many angels God created, but we do know that there are many. The author of Hebrews tells us that there are myriads, and then we see in Luke's account of the birth of Jesus that a company of angels appeared to the shepherds.

Satan—This entity has captivated man's curiosity almost from the beginning of time. He has been made into a caricature in the movies, and the subject of best-selling books, but what is the real Satan, why does he exist, and how do we fight him?

The noun satan, both in Hebrew and Greek means adversary or accuser, so Satan is the Adversary of God.

---

[62] *New American Standard Bible : 1995 Update* (LaHabra, CA: The Lockman Foundation, 1995), 2 Ki 19:35.

In the Old Testament we have our best picture in the book of Job. Satan mocks Job's faith to God so he is granted certain powers in which to torment Job and make him try to renounce God; he has no power but what God grants him. It is in the Apocrypha and other non-canonical books, do we find the malevolent Satan, and in the New Testament we find through the writings of Paul that Satan is the chief of the fallen angels who fell due to his pride (1 Tim 3:6), who was cast out of Heaven (Luke 10:18), was cast into Hell (2 Peter 2:4), and will be cast into the everlasting fire (Matthew 25:41). To get the fullest picture we have to view all of Scripture, and when we do we find Satan to be the serpent to tempted Eve in the Garden, but we have to take Genesis 3:1-5 and Revelation 12:9 together to see that. In the New Testament, Satan has many names:

> The Gospels refer to Satan as "tempter" (Matt. 4:3), "ruler of demons" (Matt. 9:34; 12:24; Mark 3:22; Luke 11:15), "evil one" (Matt. 13:38), "enemy" (Matt. 13:39), "the father of lies" (John 8:44), "a murderer" (John 8:44), and "ruler of this world" (John 12:31; 14:30; 16:11). Paul referred to him as "the god of this world" (2 Cor. 4:4), "the prince of the powers of the air" (Eph. 2:2), "the ruler of the darkness of this age" (Eph. 6:12); and "tempter" (1 Thess. 3:5). Paul warned

the Corinthians that Satan may appear as an "angel of light" (2 Cor. 11:14). In the General Epistles he is referred to as "an adversary" (1 Pet. 5:8) and "the evil one" (1 John 5:19). Revelation refers to him as "one who deceives" (Rev. 12:9), "an accuser" (Rev. 12:10), "a serpent" (Rev. 12:9), and "a dragon" (Rev. 12:3-17; 13:2, 11).[63]

Satan continues to do battle. He tempts and deceives people with lies and distortions of Scripture, with his favorite lie being that we too can be like God. This deceit has been working well for him as we see so many people fooled into believing that they are in control, and that they know what is best for them. We know the end; Satan loses and is cast into the fire pit for all eternity, the question is, how many souls he is taking with him.

Demons—While angels are mentioned often in the Old Testament, there are very few references to demons, it is in the New Testament that we see these malevolent spirits invading people. Demons were responsible for the physical and psychological problems that Jesus cured during His ministry on earth. He cast out the demons from the man in Garasene, casting them into pigs that

---

[63] Chad Brand, Charles Draper, Archie England et al., *Holman Illustrated Bible Dictionary* (Nashville, TN: Holman Bible Publishers, 2003), 419-20.

then fell off a cliff (Mark 5:1-20). Jesus cast out seven demons from Mary Magdalene (Luke 8:2ff). All manner of ailments were attributed to demon possession, but that does not negate the reality of demons. Just as Satan is real, so too demons, but they cannot inhabit a believer. John MacArthur writes:

> There is no clear example in the Bible where a demon ever inhabited or invaded a true believer. Never in the New Testament epistles are believers warned about the possibility of being inhabited by demons. Neither do we see anyone rebuking, binding, or casting demons out of a true believer. The epistles never instruct believers to cast out demons, whether from a believer or unbeliever. Christ and the apostles were the only ones who cast out demons, and in every instance the demon-possessed people were unbelievers.[64]

If you have the Holy Spirit in you, there cannot be demons; perfect good cannot coexist with evil of any sort.

---

[64] MacArthur, John. *Can Christians Be Demon Possessed?*. http://www.gty.org/resources/questions/QA191/can-christians-be-demonpossessed. Accessed 11-28-2011.

What's Next

We have explored who God is; His attributes, both incommunicable and moral, and discovered that God is a triune God, three persons who are co-existent and co-eternal who possess all the stated attributes. We have looked at His Creation, and now we will see who the Son truly is and examine the sacrifice that He made for our sake.

Study Questions:

1. Name and describe the three "omnis" of God.
2. Who are the three persons of the Trinity?
3. What are the three purposes of Creation?
4. Read through Romans 12 and 1 Corinthians 12 and find as many of the gifts of the Holy Spirit as you can. Hint: there are eighteen.
5. Find as many names for the Holy Spirit that are used in Scripture.
6. What happens when God takes His Spirit from someone? See 1 Samuel 16:12ff.

Meditation Questions:

1. Remember the life you had before the Holy Spirit acted in you. How are the fruit of the Spirit (Gal 5:22) showing in you now?

2. As you read the Bible, could you understand what God is telling without the Holy Spirit?

3. What does God's "goodness" mean to you? Read Psalm 106:1.

4. What does the fact the God is your Father mean to you? Compare Him to your biological father.

5. Read Ephesians 1 and focus on verses 4, 7, 13. What does this tell you about the Trinity?

6. Write a prayer using A.C.T.S. as a model.

CHAPTER 4

Jesus

What distinguishes Christians from every other religion is the belief that there is a second person of the Triune God that became human, suffered, died and rose again as a means of our salvation. This second person, Jesus, is not a created god or a lesser god, but fully equal in power and glory with the Father and the Holy Spirit. We touched on the sonship of Jesus in the previous chapter and we will examine what are called the offices of Jesus; Prophet, Priest and King. First, however we need to examine how Jesus is both fully God and fully man. We will look at John 1:1-18 as a basis for this discussion.

> 1 In the beginning was the Word, and the Word was with God, and the Word was God.
> 2 He was in the beginning with God.
> 3 All things came into being through Him, and apart from Him nothing came into being that has come into being.

4 In Him was life, and the life was the Light of men.

5 The Light shines in the darkness, and the darkness did not comprehend it.

6 There came a man sent from God, whose name was John.

7 He came as a witness, to testify about the Light, so that all might believe through him.

8 He was not the Light, but *he came* to testify about the Light.

9 There was the true Light which, coming into the world, enlightens every man.

10 He was in the world, and the world was made through Him, and the world did not know Him.

11 He came to His own, and those who were His own did not receive Him.

12 But as many as received Him, to them He gave the right to become children of God, *even* to those who believe in His name,

13 who were born, not of blood nor of the will of the flesh nor of the will of man, but of God.

14 And the Word became flesh, and dwelt among us, and we saw His glory, glory as of the only begotten from the Father, full of grace and truth.

15 John testified about Him and cried out, saying, "This was He of whom I said, 'He who

comes after me has a higher rank than I, for He existed before me.'"

16 For of His fullness we have all received, and grace upon grace.

17 For the Law was given through Moses; grace and truth were realized through Jesus Christ.

18 No one has seen God at any time; the only begotten God who is in the bosom of the Father, He has explained *Him.* [65]

Jesus Fully God—In verse one John writes that the Word (Jesus) was in the beginning, that He was with God and that He is God; a very definite statement about the divinity of Jesus. In verse two John tells us that Jesus was involved with all of creation saying that nothing was made apart from him; and finally in verse 18 John writes that Jesus is the only begotten Son who is with the Father now.

From just this Prolog to John's Gospel, we get a full appreciation of the divinity of Jesus; that He is co-eternal, co-powerful (omnipotent) in His creation of all things, and is, as we discussed in the previous chapter about the trinity, one with the Father. He is, as the Nicene Creed confesses, one in substance with the Father. Paul wrote in

---

[65]   *New American Standard Bible : 1995 Update* (LaHabra, CA: The Lockman Foundation, 1995), Jn 1:1–18.

Philippians 2:6 that Jesus existed "in the form of God" and the Apostle Thomas, after seeing the resurrected Jesus proclaims "My Lord and my God!"

<u>Jesus Fully Man</u>—Again we can turn to John's Prolog in verse 14 And the Word became flesh, and dwelt among us. [66] Paul, again from Philippians 2, wrote that Jesus emptied Himself and took on the form of man and humbled Himself in obedience. Jesus' humanity is shown throughout the New Testament, especially in the Gospels where we see that Jesus was born of a woman (Luke 2:7), He was hungry (Mark 11:12), He cried (John 11:35), and He died (Mt 27:50). The importance for Jesus to become human was that we needed a man to atone for man's sins.

The fact that Jesus was fully human is not the whole story; Jesus was a fully obedient human. Jesus kept the Law perfectly, and that is why He was the "spotless Lamb" that was the only sacrifice acceptable to the Father. If it was not for His obedience, then any human could have died, but in keeping with the Old Testament Law, the sacrifice had to be a spotless lamb, free from defect. Jesus, and only Jesus, filled that requirement in His life of obedience. There is no other that has lived that is truly sinless as Jesus was.

---

[66] *New American Standard Bible : 195 Update* (LaHabra, CA: The Lockman Foundation, 1995), Jn 1:14.

In Scripture we see three "offices" that Jesus fills; Prophet, Priest and King.

Jesus as Prophet—First, we have to define what a prophet is in order to see how Jesus fulfills this office perfectly. A prophet is more than a foreteller of events; one who sees into the future to let you know what is going to happen. The biblical prophet is one who speaks the divine will of God. Deuteronomy 18:18 defines the prophetic office as seen in Moses, Elijah and Elisha, but also looks forward to the fulfillment of this office in Jesus: *I will raise up a prophet from among their countrymen like you, and I will put My words in his mouth, and he shall speak to them all that I command him.* [67] This verse from Deuteronomy is quoted by Peter in Acts 3:22-23 in reference to Jesus. Jesus spoke the words of God and interpreted the will of God. Jesus distilled the Old Testament Law and Prophets into two Great Commandments. In Matthew 22:37-40 Jesus answers a question from one of the lawyers of the Pharisees:

> "'You shall love the Lord your God with all your heart, and with all your soul, and with all your mind.' "This is the great and foremost commandment. "The second is like it, 'You shall love your neighbor as yourself.' "On

---

[67] *New American Standard Bible : 1995 Update* (LaHabra, CA: The Lockman Foundation, 1995), Dt 18:18.

these two commandments depend the whole Law and the Prophets." [68]

From this we see that Jesus interpreted what God had given Moses in the desert, and in this way was a prophet who spoke the words of God. The first part of this comes from the *Shema*, or what we may consider the Jewish statement of faith from Deuteronomy 6:5 and the second part of this comes from Leviticus 19:18. Jesus, as prophet takes the words of God, interprets and becomes the medium between God and man.

The biblical prophet also performed miracles to reinforce his prophetic statements. The Gospel of Mark records eighteen miracles that Jesus performed including healing, casting out demons, and raising from the dead; all of which were a prelude to or an example for His teaching. The prophet was a teacher and Jesus taught well. In Matthew 5-7, Jesus teaches the crowds in what is known as The Sermon on the Mount, where He teaches about prayer and how to lead a right life. Lastly, Jesus did predict future events, mostly in the context of His life and His second coming. Matthew 24-25 are filled with these predictions.

---

[68] *New American Standard Bible : 1995 Update* (LaHabra, CA: The Lockman Foundation, 1995), Mt 22:37–40.

Through teachings, miracles, foretelling and interpreting God's Word and will, Jesus revealed the Father through His life, bringing us closer to a loving knowledge of God. But this is not limited to Christ's earthly ministry. In the period of the Old Testament, Jesus appeared to Abraham and others speaking for the Father. In Genesis 22:11-15 in the story of Abraham and Isaac, Jesus appears as "the Angel of the Lord." There is a definite distinction in the Old Testament between "the Angel of the Lord" and "an angel of the Lord," the later being only a messenger of God, not Jesus.

Jesus as Priest—Where a prophet was one who is God's representative to the people, a priest is the people's representative to God. Here is where we truly see Christ's two-fold nature of being full God and fully human. As being fully God and one with the Father, Jesus was able to be the "spokesman" for God, but being fully man, He can be our representative (John in his First Letter calls Jesus our Advocate, 1 John 2:1).

The functions of a priest as Scripture defines are laid out in Hebrews 5:1; here we see that a priest is called out from among his own men to be their representative, appointed by God, active in the things of God, makes intercession for his people (Heb 7:25), and blesses them in the name of God (Lev 9:22); but the most important function of the priest was to offer a sacrifice for sins. This was usually in the way of animal sacrifice as can be seen in Genesis 8:19-20 where Noah offers up a sacrifice of some of the clean animals as a burnt offering to God. These offerings are considered expiatory (atoning) and were laid out for the Hebrews in the book of Leviticus. We will examine the doctrine of the Atonement later in this chapter, simply put Jesus, as our High Priest offered up the perfect sacrifice in atonement for our sins; He did this by offering His own body as an offering (Eph 5:2).

Jesus as King—Being fully God and co-equal with the Father, Jesus is enthroned above. He reigns as King over His people, His Church. In a prophetic psalm, the writer of Psalm 2:6 wrote about Christ "But as for Me, I have installed My King Upon Zion, My holy mountain." [69] Jesus in King over a spiritual Kingdom, He does not (at least not yet) reign on earth. We will discuss Christ's earthly kingdom in Chapter 9 when we discuss the end times. Entering into the Kingdom of Christ is through regeneration, or new birth. John 3:5 Jesus answered, "Truly, truly, I say to you, unless one is born of water and the Spirit he cannot enter into the kingdom of God." [70]

---

[69] *New American Standard Bible : 1995 Update* (LaHabra, CA: The Lockman Foundation, 1995), Ps 2:6.

[70] *New American Standard Bible : 1995 Update* (LaHabra, CA: The Lockman Foundation, 1995), Jn 3:5.

Jesus is also King over the universe. He administers all things for His glory and for the good of the Church.

> As King of the universe the Mediator so guides the destinies of individuals, of social groups, and of nations, as to promote the growth, the gradual purification, and final perfection of the people which He has redeemed with His blood. [71]

All things come under the rule of Christ, Psalm 2:8 shows how Christ was given all things to rule over.

Prophecies Pointing to Jesus—In the Old Testament there are about three hundred separate prophecies regarding the birth, life, suffering, death and resurrection of Jesus. In Psalm 22 alone there are four prophecies pointing to Jesus (vv. 1, 7, 8, 18). Isaiah had the most with fourteen prophecies (9:7; 7:14; 11:2; 42:1; 41:4; 44:3-8; 50:5-6; 52:14; 53:5-6; 53:7; 53:9; 53:12; 61:1) and there can be found prophecies or types of Christ in almost every book of the Old Testament, which shows the reliability of Scripture.

Jesus' birth was prophesied as being born in Bethlehem (Micah 5:2-5), of a virgin (Isaiah 7:13-14) and in the lineage

---

[71] Berkhof, Louis. Systematic Theolgy. Grand Rapids: William B. Eerdmans Publishing Company. 1996. 410.

of David (Isaiah 9:7). The prophecy of His Triumphal Entry is described in John 12:12-16 and His crucifixion in Psalm 22:16; 18, Psalm 69:20-22 Zechariah 12:10 and Exodus 12:46. Some of these prophecies were proclaimed 1200 years before Jesus' birth.

Heresies Regarding Jesus—Ever since Jesus ascended into Heaven, there have been heretical beliefs about His deity and His humanity, ranging from the mild to the totally bizarre. Here are a few:

- Arianism—This one came about in the late third century and was one of the reasons why the Council of Nicea was called. In this belief, Arius, an Egyptian minister, denies the full deity of Christ, that He is a lesser God who was not from the beginning as John wrote, but a created god.
- Docetism—This is the belief that Jesus only appeared to have a human body, and that He only appeared to have died on the cross. This heresy was brought forth by a group called the Gnostics. It was their belief that anything material (i.e. body) was evil, therefore Christ could be God and have an evil body.
- Monophysitism—This heresy denies the dual nature of Christ and holds that the human nature of Christ was taken up by the divine nature and made into some sort of third type of nature.

The Atonement

One of the terms that we hear in churches that gives us the most problems is the word atonement; what does it mean, why did we need it and how was it accomplished in Christ?

<u>What does it mean?</u>—One way of looking at this doctrine is to take the word for what to is: at-one-ment; in other words to be reconciled. The concept atonement comes from the Old Testament sacrifices as laid out in the book of Leviticus; it is God's way of re-entering into a right relationship with Him. It is purely an act of God and not of man. It is initiated by God; He gave the Israelites a means of atonement in the burnt offerings and in the New Testament, He gave His only Son. It is God's way of making things right between Him and us. We cannot do it, so only He can.

Atonement is an offering for sin. In the Old Testament, we see in Leviticus 16 the prescription for the Day of Atonement, or as it is called Yom Kippur. The high priest could enter, only on that day, into the Holy of Holies, to offer a sacrifice for the sins of the nation of Israel. Jesus as our High Priest, made this sacrifice, once for all, in fulfillment of His priestly duties. The sacrifice that He offered was not bulls or goats, but His life. Jesus' sacrifice was for the sins of those who put their faith in Him, both past and future. There is no need for the atonement sacrifice to be repeated as it is all sufficient to cover all sins of those who call on His name.

When we talk about atonement there are two other words that are used in regard to this doctrine; both of which can be confusing, and both are words that we do not use in everyday conversation: expiation and propitiation. These words you may hear if you attend a Bible study, or if your pastor slips one of these into a sermon. Expiation, found only once in the New American Standard Version (NASB95) in Numbers 35:33, and propitiation is found only four times, all in the New Testament (Ro 3:25; Heb 2:17; 1 John 2:2; 4:10). So the use of these words, while not commonplace have important impact on our understanding of what the atonement is. Some translations, even some teachers will equate these two words, giving them the same meaning, but there are significant differences that need to be noted.

Expiation—Expiation is the process by which our sins are covered where propitiation is the appeasement of the offended party; in our case God. It is through propitiation that our sins are expiated (confused yet?) 1 John 4:14 *In this is love, not that we loved God, but that He loved us and sent His Son to be the propitiation for our sins.* [72] Paul

---

[72] *New American Standard Bible : 1995 Update* (LaHabra, CA: The Lockman Foundation, 1995), 1 Jn 4:10.

here is writing that God initiated the atonement by sending His Son as a sacrifice to appease His wrath, so that our sins would be covered. The two words are sometimes used mistakenly as the same but "Expiation properly has a thing as its object. We may expiate a crime, or a sin. Propitiation is a personal word. We propitiate a person rather than a sin."[73] Our sins are expiated by the blood of Jesus; they are covered, giving us the appearance of righteousness.

> Guilt is said to be expiated when it is visited with punishment falling on a substitute. Expiation is made for our sins when they are punished not in ourselves but in another who consents to stand in our room. It is that by which reconciliation is effected. Sin is thus said to be "covered" by vicarious satisfaction.[74]

Propitiation—The wrath of God is not something we like to talk about because we get the pagan idea of an angry god throwing thunder bolts at bad people. We have the image of Zeus sitting on Mount Olympus, angry about

---

[73] L. L. Morris, "Expiation", in New Bible Dictionary, ed. D. R. W. Wood, I. H. Marshall, A. R. Millard et al., 3rd ed., 353 (Leicester, England; Downers Grove, IL: InterVarsity Press, 1996).

[74] M. G. Easton, Easton's Bible Dictionary (Oak Harbor, WA: Logos Research Systems, Inc., 1996).

something; all in a rage, but that is not our God. God does not get angry for any trivial reason; His anger is with sin.

> For there is nothing capricious or arbitrary about the holy God. Nor is he ever irascible, malicious, spiteful or vindictive. His anger is neither mysterious nor irrational. It is never unpredictable, but always predictable, because it is provoked by evil, and evil alone. The wrath of God...is his steady, unrelenting, unremitting, uncompromising antagonism to evil in all its forms and manifestations. [75]

God's wrath does need to be assuaged; the problem is that nothing that we could do could assuage the wrath that we deserve. No amount of works, good deeds, constant Bible reading, going to church every day, giving everything we own to the poor; nothing that is of us can even begin to lessen the anger that God has at the evil we do, so there has to be some sort of sacrifice that would be acceptable to God. God, in His graciousness, provides the propitiatory sacrifice; His Son. In Romans 3:25, Paul writes "God presented him as a sacrifice" (NIV). Christ was the perfect sacrifice that appeased the wrath of God

---

[75] Stott, John R.W. *The Cross of Christ*. Downers Grove, IL: IVP Books, 2006. 171.

"not that we loved God, but that He loved us and sent His Son to be the propitiation for our sins."(1 John 4:10) Or a Stott writes "God does not love us because Christ died for us; Christ died for us because God loved us. If it was God's wrath that needed to be propitiated, it was God's love that did the propitiating."[76]

How the Atonement was accomplished—Let's do a simple re-cap of the whole scene: 1) because of our sin we face the wrath of God—Ro 6:23. 2) There is nothing that we could offer that could appease this angry God (propitiation)—Ps 49:7. 3) God wants a relationship with us.—John 3:16. 4) God initiates the process of covering our sins (expiation)—Ro 4:10. 5) Jesus is the perfect sacrifice that accomplishes this.—Ro 3:25

As we read through the Old Testament there are ways in which God provided ways to atone for the sins of the nation of Israel, through the shedding of the blood of animals. Hebrews 9:22 *And according to the Law, one may almost say, all things are cleansed with blood, and without shedding of blood there is no forgiveness.* [77] Since Jesus is our High Priest, He, and He alone is capable of offering a sacrifice for our sins that would cover them past

---

[76] Stott. 172.

[77] *New American Standard Bible : 1995 Update* (LaHabra, CA: The Lockman Foundation, 1995), Heb 9:22.

and future, but it did come at a cost. In order to uphold the Old Testament Law, and to fulfill that Law, Jesus shed His blood as an atoning sacrifice for us. Just as the high priests in the Temple would offer an unblemished animal as a sacrifice, our High Priest offers Himself, unblemished by sin as an offering.

Study Questions:

1. What is the word that John uses for Jesus in John 1?
2. Read Hebrews 9. What does it say about the difference between the old covenant that God had made with Israel and the new covenant through Christ?
3. Define atonement, expiation and propitiation.
4. What are the three offices of Christ?
5. How many names for Christ can you find in the New Testament?

Meditation Questions:

1. Read John 1:1-18. How is Jesus portrayed?
2. The book of Hebrews speaks about Jesus as High Priest; what does that mean to you?
3. Why can't you atone for your own sins?

CHAPTER 5

Man and Sin

Man, us, humans, men and women, boys and girls, each of us is created in the image of God, not a exact copy, but in the image of God. We were created, not because God was lonely, not because God needed anything in the way of amusement (though when He is not weeping over what man has done, He probably is amused as to how far we have gone in messing things up) but because to create man, it brought glory to Him. Let's look at God creativeness in forming man as a vehicle for His love.

Creation—In Genesis 1:26 there is a difference in tone and in style from the rest of the creation story. Up till now, God by divine fiat created the inanimate objects (sun, moon, stars, and plants) and the animals that will be needed to help man live. When it comes to the creation of man, God uses an "executive divine counsel." In other words, the Triune God works together in creating man. He consults with Himself to form man in His image; "let

US make man in OUR image" (author's emphasis). John Calvin in his commentary on Genesis wrote:

> so now, for the purpose of commending to our attention the dignity of our nature, he, in taking counsel concerning the creation of man, testifies that he is about to undertake something great and wonderful.[78]

As we discussed the Trinity, we saw how the plural form of the pronoun is argued to be that of perfection or that the plural form indicated majesty or regalness, but it has since the beginning of the Church been acknowledged as being the Triune God at work.

Unique to man, God created us in His image; that image being personal; we are like God in that we can think, we can manage the things that God gave us (have dominion over...), be creative and, only before the Fall, be morally perfect. Paul wrote in 1 Corinthians 11:7 that we are "the image and glory of God." That glory is the personality that God gave us. Just as the Trinity has three persons, we too have an individual personality in which we relate to each other and to God. Another way of saying this is that each one of us has a soul. In Genesis 2:7, the second account

---

[78] John Calvin, *Calvin's Commentaries* (Galaxie Software, 2002; 2002), Ge 1:1.

of the creation, God breathed life into man. God did not breathe into any other animal, but only to man, that we would have God in us; His image implanted on us. Later we will discuss how the image and glory of God became tainted.

Male and Female—In the creation story God made man. Genesis 1:27 say that both male and female were created, men and women were created in God's image. Woman was not created inferior to man or man inferior to woman. God created both in His image, perfect and the representation of His glory, but through the millennia, things changed. First, let's look at the biblical roles of men and women, then the corruption of those roles.

Biblical roles—As stated, there was no difference in the creative process of God in the making of men and women; both created in His image and for His glory. Then, because of the Fall and the perversion of the human nature by sin, the roles of men and women became hierarchical with the woman being subservient to the man. As we look through Scripture, we see that God uses both men and women for His plan.

Old Testament—It is obvious that sin has perverted the roles in which men and women were created. God made both man and woman in His image, and women played an important role in God's plan in the Old Testament. While by the time of Jesus, a woman's role and position was that of home-maker and mother, early Jewish history had women in important positions. Deborah was a judge. Judges in post-Exodus Israel were the leaders of the nation. Judges 2:18 *When the Lord raised up judges for them, the Lord was with the judge and delivered them from the hand of their enemies all the days of the judge; for the Lord was moved to pity by their groaning because of those who oppressed and afflicted them.* [79] Generals and leaders all went to Deborah for advice; Huldah was a prophetess who the high priests under king Josiah came for advice, and Merriam, the sister of Aaron and Moses led worship in the desert. As history evolved, women became less influential in Hebrew culture. During the earthly ministry of Jesus a woman could not enter the Temple or speak at a synagogue.

New Testament—What Jesus did in His encounters with women was radical for the day. He spoke to women, taught them, ate with them and counted women as some of His closest friends. In the well-known parable of Jesus and the women caught in adultery, Jesus did not condemn the woman, but showed her accusers that they all were sinful and had no right to judge. An important missing part of the story is the man. In adultery, according to Leviticus 20:10,

---

[79] *New American Standard Bibl: 1995 Update* (LaHabra, CA: The Lockman Foundation, 1995), Jdg 2:18.

both the man and the woman were to be put to death for the crime, yet the man was not brought before Jesus, only the woman. Jesus had women as disciples. In Luke's Gospel, he names three women who supported Jesus in His ministry. They were Mary Magdalene, Joanna, and Susanna (Luke 8:1-3).

Many people point to the letter of Paul to diminish the roles of women. Particularly troublesome is in Paul's letter to the Ephesians:

> *Wives, be subject to your own husbands, as to the Lord. For the husband is the head of the wife, as Christ also is the head of the church, He Himself being the Savior of the body.* [80] Eph 5:23-24

It is in our interpretation of the word "head" that gets us in trouble. In the ancient Greek, the word for head does not mean authority, but source, or responsibility for. So when Paul writes that the husband is head of the wife, he is writing that the husband has a responsibility for the wife. In writing about the roles of men in marriage, John Piper wrote:

---

[80] *New American Standard Bible : 1995 Update* (LaHabra, CA: The Lockman Foundation, 1995), Eph 5:22–23.

> You should feel the greater responsibility
> to take the lead in things of the Spirit; you
> should lead the family in a life of prayer; in
> the study of God's Word, and in worship; you
> should lead in giving the family a vision of its
> meaning and missions; you should take the
> lead in shaping tej moral fabric of the home
> and in governing its happy peace.[81]

Paul also in misunderstood in his writings about women in ministry. In 1 Corinthians 14:34, Paul says that women should not be allowed to speak in church. If this were so, why then did Paul acknowledge and thank so many women in Romans 16 who Paul calls co-workers, including Junia, whom he calls an apostle? Context is so important when reading Scripture, and a basic knowledge of history can also prove invaluable. Remember, at this time in history, a woman was not taught the Torah, so for her to speak, she would have been speaking from ignorance. That is why Paul says that she should go to her husband at home to be taught FIRST. Paul writes about equality of men and women and races and nationalities in Galatians 3:28 *There is neither Jew nor Greek, there is neither slave nor*

---

[81] Piper, John. *Desiring God: Meditations of a Christian Hedonist.* Colorado Springs, CO: Multnomah Books, 2003. 219.

free man, there is neither male nor female; for you are all one in Christ Jesus. [82]

Historical Abuse—Since sin crept in, man has found a need in ruling over women, not as God created, but is a relationship that is unequal. Beginning with Israel being influenced by the patriarchal pagan cultures to the misinterpretation of Scripture, women have become subservient in society and the Church. But as we look rightly at Scripture we see a different story. Women have been prohibited from leadership in the Church because of the misinterpretation of Paul, but recently women have been assuming a rightful place within the church as pastors, teachers, and deacons. [83]

Sin—Now it's time to address the elephant in the room: sin. A while back I officiated at a funeral for an elderly woman and during the message I spoke about why it was important for this woman to have accepted Christ as Savior; that by this faith in Jesus, the woman was assured of a place in eternity with Him, and that it was through Jesus that her sins were atoned for. After the service a granddaughter came up to me and said her

---

[82] *New American Standard Bible : 1995 Update* (LaHabra, CA: The Lockman Foundation, 1995), Ga 3:28.

[83] For more information on biblical equality go to Christians for Biblical Equality at www.cbeinternational.org or read *Called and Gifted* by Sharon Cairns Mann.

grandmother never sinned! I tried to explain that we all sin but this young woman would not associate sin with her grandmother, obviously not understanding the nature of sin, or what the Bible tells us about it.

So what is sin? According to the Westminster Shorter Catechism:

Q. 14. What is sin?

A. Sin is any want of conformity unto, or transgression of, the law of God.[84]

Anytime that we do not follow God's law, we sin, so let's expand that a bit as see what God's law requires of us. Jesus broke down God's law into two basic principles. In a conversation with a expert of the Law, Jesus was asked:

"Teacher, which is the great commandment in the Law?" And He said to him, "'You shall love the Lord your God with all your heart, and with all your soul, and with all your mind.' "This is the great and foremost commandment. "The second is like it, 'You shall love your neighbor as yourself.' "On

---

[84] Westminster Shorter Catechism. http://www.reformed.org/documents/index.html?mainframe=http://www.reformed.org/documents/WSC_frames.html. Accessed 1-17-12.

these two commandments depend the whole Law and the Prophets."[85]

Whenever we do not love God with all our heart, soul and mind, and do not love our neighbor as ourselves, we sin. Think about this for a minute. If we come to church or read the Bible or pray half-heartedly, we are sinning. If we do not love our neighbor, not only not doing something to someone, but not doing something for someone, we sin. You can see why we need a Savior, it is impossible for us not to sin. Augustine, the 4th century Church Father, wrote that man, when in Eden was able not to sin, but after the Fall, man was unable not to sin. By the work of Jesus, those who put their faith in Him will at the resurrection be unable to sin. Because of our sinful nature, and without the help of the Holy Spirit, we are unable not to sin. In Reformed theology this is called the total depravity of man.

We all sin. It is a cold hard fact that cannot be denied. John wrote in 1 John 1:10 *If we claim we have not sinned, we make him out to be a liar and his word has no place in our lives.* [86] It is what we do from thjis point on that is important. First, we have to recognize that we do not and

---

[85] *New American Standard Bible: 1995 Update* (LaHabra, CA: The Lockman Foundation, 1995), Mt 22:36–40.

[86] The Holy Bible: New International Version, 1 Jn 1:10 (Grand Rapids, MI: Zondervan, 1984).

cannot live a sinless life; only Jesus in His perfection was able to do this. Secondly, with that realization, we have to rely on a Savior to keep us from the punishment that we deserve; Hell. We cannot redeem ourselves from our sin, that is why Jesus came, suffered and died, that we can have His righteousness. Proverbs 20:9 *Who can say, "I have cleansed my heart, I am pure from my sin"?* [87]

The Fall—We have seen this word used and capitalized in many places so far, but what really was the Fall, and how are we free from its consequences? Genesis 3 tells the story of Adam and Eve being tempted by the serpent to eat of the fruit of the Tree of Knowledge of Good and Evil. Adam sinned by disobeying God, and that sin has been imputed (transferred) to us because Adam is our common ancestor. This is called Original Sin, that this imputed sin comes from our origin; Adam. It is a fall from grace, a falling away from God's presence and being under the influence of Satan. But God gives us a way out of the effects of sin, which is death. In Genesis 3:15 God promises a way out.

> *And I will put enmity between you and the woman, and between your seed and her*

---

[87]   New American Standard Bible: 1995 Update, Pr 20:9 (LaHabra, CA: The Lockman Foundation, 1995).

seed; He shall bruise you on the head, and
you shall bruise him on the heel."[88]

This is what is called by theologians the *Protoevangelium* or the first announcement of the good news of salvation found in Jesus. The seed of the woman is Jesus, who came in human form as an atoning sacrifice. In this we see the temporary, non-lethal injury to the seed of the woman. Jesus was crucified, but rose again to defeat death. The serpent sustained a lethal injury, prophesying the death of Satan and his rule over men.

Just as we all inherit original sin, that because of one man we all face death, so too through one Man we have life. Paul wrote in Letter to the Romans:

Therefore, just as through one man sin
entered into the world, and death through
sin, and so death spread to all men, because
all sinned—But the free gift is not like the
transgression. For if by the transgression of
the one the many died, much more did the
grace of God and the gift by the grace of the

---

[88]   *New American Standard Bible : 1995 Update* (LaHabra, CA: The Lockman Foundation, 1995), Ge 3:15.

> *one Man, Jesus Christ, abound to the many.*
> *(Romans 5:12; 15)* [89]

The 3rd century Church Father, Tertullian wrote: "It was necessary that Christ would come forth for the salvation of man in that same condition of flesh into which man had entered ever since his condemnation."

The Price of Sin—We are told in the story of the fall that there was a price to be paid for the sin of Adam; relationship issues (Yet your desire will be for your husband, And he will rule over you."), [90] pain ("I will greatly multiply Your pain in childbirth, In pain you will bring forth children), [91] hard work (In toil you will eat of it All the days of your life), [92] and death (For you are dust, And to dust you shall return). Because we are descendants of Adam, we have inherited all these ills and because of this we also have inherited Adam's sin of pride. In our pride we believe that we can do what we want, when we want without consequences; that sin is a fool's concept, and

---

[89] *New American Standard Bible: 1995 Update* (LaHabra, CA: The Lockman Foundation, 1995), Ro 5:15.

[90] *New American Standard Bible: 1995 Update* (LaHabra, CA: The Lockman Foundation, 1995), Ge 3:16.

[91] *New American Standard Bible: 1995 Update* (LaHabra, CA: The Lockman Foundation, 1995), Ge 3:16.

[92] *New American Standard Bible: 1995 Update* (LaHabra, CA: The Lockman Foundation, 1995), Ge 3:17.

that God is for the weak minded. Without Jesus' work on the cross, we would continue in this way, and suffer the effects of that as eternal damnation. I know that this is not a politically correct concept, that God would punish sinners for eternity, but that is what He says.

> *to those who by perseverance in doing good seek for glory and honor and immortality, eternal life; but to those who are selfishly ambitious and do not obey the truth, but obey unrighteousness, wrath and indignation. (Romans 2:7-8)*[93]

Paul, in this letter to the Roman Church later wrote; *For the wages of sin is death, but the free gift of God is eternal life in Christ Jesus our Lord.* (Ro 6:23)[94] The price of sin is death, but because God, by His mercy and grace, called us to be His, we have life eternal.

Study Questions:

1. Read Genesis 1-3; how did Satan deceive Eve?
2. What are the results of the Fall as laid out in Genesis 3:14-19?

---

[93] *New American Standard Bible: 1995 Update* (LaHabra, CA: The Lockman Foundation, 1995), Ro 2:7–8.

[94] *New American Standard Bible: 1995 Update* (LaHabra, CA: The Lockman Foundation, 1995), Ro 6:23.

3. What were some of the roles women had in the Bible and does that agree with the roles of women in the Church today?

Meditation Questions:

1. What does it mean to you to be created in God's image?
2. What does it mean to sin?
3. Memorize Romans 6:23 and meditate on the "free gift."

CHAPTER 6

Salvation

And we know that God causes all things to work together for good to those who love God, to those who are called according to His purpose.

For those whom He foreknew, He also predestined to become conformed to the image of His Son, so that He would be the firstborn among many brethren; and these whom He predestined, He also called; and these whom He called, He also justified; and these whom He justified, He also glorified.
Romans 8:28-30 [95]

We have seen from the previous chapter that man, because of the Fall of Adam, lives in a state of sin, with

---

[95] *New American Standard Bible : 1995 Update* (LaHabra, CA: The Lockman Foundation, 1995), Ro 8:28–30.

death being the conclusion. So, when we say that we are in need of salvation, we are speaking about being delivered from this fate of eternal damnation and death into an eternal life in the presence of God. In every other religion, salvation is dependent on what man does. In Judaism, salvation is brought about by strictly obeying the 613 commandments that are found in the Hebrew Bible. In Hinduism; "Hindus believe in karma, the law of cause and effect by which each individual creates his own destiny by his thoughts, words and deeds. Hindus believe that the soul reincarnates, evolving through many births until all karmas have been resolved, and moksha, liberation from the cycle of rebirth, is attained. Not a single soul will be deprived of this destiny."[96] Islamic salvation is through five pillars that are to be obeyed: 1) Shahadah; There is no God but Allah and Muhammad is his messenger; 2) Salat: the practice of praying five times a day a times set by Allah; 3) Zarkat is the compulsory giving of a set amount of wealth, cash, gold, silver and commercial items to charity; 4) Sawm is fasting during Ramadan; and 5) Hajj; Muslims from all ethnic groups, social class, color and culture stand together in front of the Kaaba and pray together (pilgrimage). [97] Only in Christianity is our salvation not dependent on our actions, but by the free gift of God.

---

[96] _. *Nine Beliefs of Hinduism.* http://www.himalayanacademy.com/basics/nineb/. Accessed 1-26-2012.

[97] _. *Islam Beliefs.* http://www.beliefs-in-islam.com/. Accessed 1-26-2012.

For by grace you have been saved through faith; and that not of yourselves, it is the gift of God; not as a result of works, so that no one may boast. (Eph 2:8-9) [98]

There are two words, or concepts in the above verse that need some explaining.

Grace—Let's start with a working definition of grace first, then we can expand on the meaning and application of grace.

It is God's free, sovereign, undeserved favour or love to man, in his state of sin and guilt, which manifests itself in the forgiveness of sin and deliverance from its penalty.[99]

A free gift from God; not dependent on anything we do or could do, but because of His love for us. There are two types of grace that God extends; common and special.

Common Grace—Common grace is that which God extends to all His creatures, both good and evil; believers

[98] *New American Standard Bible : 1995 Update* (LaHabra, CA: The Lockman Foundation, 1995), Eph 2:8–9.

[99] Berkhof, Louis. Systematic Theology. Grand Rapids: William B. Eerdmans Publishing Company. 1996. 427.

and pagans. Common grace is the gift of God that keeps this world turning, the sun shining, and the rain falling. Without common grace, the world would be destroyed. We saw what happened when God withdrew His grace on most of the world when He caused the earth to flood. All living things were destroyed except the few that He, by His special grace, called to re-inhabit the earth. Common grace is what restrains evil from entirely taking over the world, and it is that common grace that God extends to all people that allows even unbelievers to do good works. Ps 145:9 *The Lord is good to all, And His mercies are over all His works.* [100]

Special Grace—This grace is also called uncommon grace or saving grace. This is that unmerited gift of God that He bestows on those He calls to be His. It is this grace by which we are spared the eternal torment of Hell and given a life in the presence of God. This special grace is the means of our salvation; that God would love us enough to extend His mercy or His favor on us and bring us into a relationship with Him through His Son by the power of the Holy Spirit. The work of the Holy Spirit in this special grace is what called election.

---

[100] *New American Standard Bible : 1995 Update* (LaHabra, CA: The Lockman Foundation, 1995), Ps 145:9.

Election—I will admit that this can be a controversial topic, and that not all Christians agree with the premise of election, but let's start with a definition:

> An act of God before creation in which He chose some people to be saved, not on account of any foreseen merit in them, but only because of His sovereign good pleasure.[101]

You can see why this may be a bit controversial, that God would choose some to be saved and not others. When we look at this, we have to look at who God is and who we are; God is perfectly holy, and we as Paul wrote in Romans 3:23 *for all have sinned and fall short of the glory of God.* [102] So for God to choose any to spend eternity with Him is an act of grace. Since we are all sinners, we all should suffer the same fate; death, but God, for His good pleasure, elects that some will be saved. This election process began before the earth was formed. In Paul's letter to the Ephesians, he begins this letter with this idea:

> *Blessed be the God and Father of our Lord*
> *Jesus Christ, who has blessed us with every*

---

[101] Grudem, Wayne. *Bible Doctrine: Essential Teachings of the Christian Faith.* Grand Rapids: Zondervan publishing House. 1999. 483.

[102] *New American Standard Bible : 1995 Update* (LaHabra, CA: The Lockman Foundation, 1995), Ro 3:23.

spiritual blessing in the heavenly places in Christ, just as He chose us in Him before the foundation of the world, that we would be holy and blameless before Him. [103] (Ephesians 1:3-4)

As we look through John's Gospel we hear the words of Jesus giving this doctrine of election some clarifying. Jesus was teaching and He told the crowd that:

"No one can come to Me unless the Father who sent Me draws him; and I will raise him up on the last day."[104]

It is the Father who, through the work of the Holy Spirit, draws us to His Son Jesus. This was determined long before we did anything good or bad, but because of God's love. You may be thinking to yourself that this is a bit arbitrary and that God should save all people, or at least give them the choice of accepting this grace or not; and there are those who do believe that when Jesus died on the cross He did so for all people to be saved, but Scripture does not bear that out. To call God unfair in choosing some and not others is a misunderstanding

---

[103] *New American Standard Bible: 1995 Update* (LaHabra, CA: The Lockman Foundation, 1995), Eph 1:3–4.

[104] *New American Standard Bible: 1995 Update* (LaHabra, CA: The Lockman Foundation, 1995), Jn 6:44.

of what He is accomplishing. We have to go back to who we are and the verse form Romans 3:23; we are all sinners deserving nothing in the eyes of God but eternal damnation; that God in His mercy calls any to be saved is a miracle in itself.

The doctrine of election was never really disputed until the sixteenth century by Jacobus Arminius (1560-1609) who believe that the human will should have priority in the decision of salvation. We have seen a few passages from Scripture, and we can appeal to the early Church Fathers like Augustine and the reformers like Luther and Calvin. Irenaeus, a second century Church Father wrote:

> "When the number is completed that He had predetermined in His own counsel, all those who have been enrolled for life will rise again."[105]

God's saving grace is through this process of election; without being elect before the foundations of the world, this special grace would not have been bestowed on us.

Faith—So we come back to the verse for Ephesians that tells us that we are saved by grace through faith. What is

---

[105] Bercot, David W. ed. *A Dictionary of Early Christian Beliefs.* Peabody: Hendrickson Publishers, Inc. 1998. 293.

faith, faith in what, and how do we get faith?. Again, let's start with a definition; this one directly from Scripture:

> *Now faith is the assurance of things hoped for, the conviction of things not seen.* (Hebrews 11:1)[106]

Faith is trusting God to do what He says He will do.

> *and being fully assured that what God had promised, He was able also to perform.* (Romans 4:21) [107]

God tells us, through His Spirit and His Word, that we will have eternal life; that we were chosen to be His sons and daughters and with Jesus, heirs to the Kingdom of God (Heaven). Our faith is not built on suppositions, but on the promises that God had made to us, and the fulfillment of past promises throughout history.

Faith is not something that we decide one day to have, at least not faith in God. Our sinful nature does not allow us to have faith in anything but ourselves; faith in God cannot occur in a sinful state. Now you think that that verse from

---

[106] *New American Standard Bible : 1995 Update* (LaHabra, CA: The Lockman Foundation, 1995), Heb 11:1.

[107] *New American Standard Bible : 1995 Update* (LaHabra, CA: The Lockman Foundation, 1995), Ro 4:21.

Ephesians no longer makes sense, but the miracle in this is that it is all from God. We are saved by grace; that unmerited gift of eternal life, through faith. But I just said that we do not have faith, so how can we be saved through something that we do not have? Hebrews 12:2a tells us *"...fixing our eyes on Jesus, the author and perfecter of faith."*[108] Jesus is the author of our faith, we have faith because Jesus gave us that faith. The Triune God gives us everything that we need for eternal life; first the gift of that life and second the faith by which we accept that gift. The Holy Spirit is involved in our faith also, 1 Corinthians 12:7 tells us that faith is a gift from the Spirit.

Our faith is a gift by the Author, Jesus, and the giver, the Holy Spirit, but God uses different means by which we are gifted with faith. Both John in John 20:31 and Paul in his letter to Timothy in 2 Timothy 3:15 tell us that faith come from Scriptures and John, Paul and Luke wrote that faith comes through preaching. But primarily it is a gift. Abraham had faith in a God who had yet defined Himself through the Law or any other Scriptures, but according to Genesis 15:6, and again quoted by Paul in Romans 4:3 *"Then he believed in the LORD; and He reckoned it to him as righteousness."* [109] Abraham believed God and

---

[108] *New American Standard Bible : 1995 Update* (LaHabra, CA: The Lockman Foundation, 1995), Heb 12:2.

[109] *New American Standard Bible : 1995 Update* (LaHabra, CA: The Lockman Foundation, 1995), Ge 15:6.

His promises, and believed IN God. He had faith, and because of that faith became the father of a great nation.

Born Again—we often hear about the "born again" Christians. They're in the news, a subset in polls, and some consider them to be a political force, bit what does it mean to be born again? Jesus answered this question when a ruler of the Jews named Nicodemus asked how we can be born again. Here is the story from John's Gospel:

> *Now there was a man of the Pharisees, named Nicodemus, a ruler of the Jews;*
>
> *this man came to Jesus by night and said to Him, "Rabbi, we know that You have come from God as a teacher; for no one can do these signs that You do unless God is with him." Jesus answered and said to him, "Truly, truly, I say to you, unless one is born again he cannot see the kingdom of God." Nicodemus said to him, "How can a man be born when he is old? He cannot enter a second time into his mother's womb and be born, can he?" Jesus answered, "Truly, truly, I say to you, unless one is born of water and the Spirit he cannot enter into the kingdom of God. "That which is born of the flesh is flesh, and that which is born of the Spirit is*

spirit. "Do not be amazed that I said to you, 'You must be born again.[110](John 3:1-7)

Being "born again" means that you are a new person in Christ; the old self died off and a new self lives. It is from the Triune God; all three persons are involved in your re-birth. Peter in 1 Peter 1:3 writes it is from the Father, 1 John 2:29 says that it is from Christ, and Titus 3:5 claims it is the work of the Holy Spirit. As you can see this is a collaborative work among the three persons in the Godhead. According to His divine counsel (that means all three involved) God, by grace, through the faith that He has given you, causes you to be re-born in Him.

So how does this happen, and can you identify when it happened to you? As I said before this is a work of God, not by anything that we have done or could do, but by His grace and mercy causes us to be re-born in Him, that we can be called His children. When it happens is entirely individual. For some, it was a gradual awareness of God's grace in them; they never did not know God's love. For others, it was an experience that the day and the hour are remembered the rest of their lives. Some came forward on an "altar call" where because of the preaching of the Word, God stirred something in a heart that caused them

---

[110] *New American Standard Bible : 1995 Update* (LaHabra, CA: The Lockman Foundation, 1995), Jn 3:1–7.

to immediately go before the preacher and repent of their sins and call Jesus Lord. Some have had their conversion experience alone in desperation, when they hit bottom because of drugs or alcohol, and they cried out to Jesus for help. Then there are those, like me who came to know Jesus through the reading of His Word, and the Word penetrated my heart causing me to give my life to Him. In each experience it was God working in you to make you new. Paul wrote in 2 Corinthians 5:17 *Therefore if anyone is in Christ, he is a new creature; the old things passed away; behold, new things have come.* [111]

Your re-birth from God makes you a new creature, you are regenerated, but Paul writes that the old things have passed away; you don't feel that do you? The old self, that heart that could not do anything but sin, is now a heart that can resist sin, though we stumble all the time.

It is humanly manageable to make decisions of the will for Christ. No supernatural power is required to pray prayers, sign cards, walk aisles, or even stop sleeping around. Those are good. They just don't prove that anything spiritual has happened. Christian conversion, on the other hand,

---

[111] *New American Standard Bible : 1995 Update* (LaHabra, CA: The Lockman Foundation, 1995), 2 Co 5:17.

is a supernatural, radical thing. The heart is changed. And the evidence of it in not just new decisions, but new affections, new feelings.[112]

Sanctification—we get frustrated almost daily after we are 'born-again' because we continue to sin; to fall down on our walk with God. We expected that once we gave our hearts to Jesus and call Him Lord, we would not continue in the past ways; we would automatically quit drinking and never have an urge again or we could quit smoking cold turkey, or never again be tempted by pornography or any of the other temptations in this world. These frustrations often lead to doubt, and that is exactly what the Evil One wants. We need to first understand what sanctification is and how does it work in our re-born lives.

When we are re-born, we are not magically transformed in to this perfect creature that does not sin and is not tempted. We are however transformed form a child of the Devil to a child of God. (More on our adoption later.) Our hearts are transformed, and now instead of not being able to do anything but sin we now have the ability not to sin. Notice I said the ability not the perfection of not sinning. This is a process; a long road that we must walk until

---

[112] Piper, John. *Desiring God: Meditations of a Christian Hedonist.* Colorado Springs, CO: Multnomah Books, 2003. 89.

we are called up at the final resurrection and are MADE perfect. Until then we are on a bumpy road with pitfalls and rabbit trails that can lead us astray. *Easton's Bible Dictionary* defines sanctification as:

> the work of the Holy Spirit bringing the whole nature more and more under the influences of the new gracious principles implanted in the soul in regeneration. In other words, sanctification is the carrying on to perfection the work begun in regeneration, and it extends to the whole man.[113]

When we were born-again, the Holy Spirit began a new work in us, a work that will last a lifetime, but with His help we are better able to resist temptation and sin.

There is a second part of sanctification that again, is the work of God; we are separated, set apart for His use. To "sanctify" means to set apart; to separate from the rest of the world. Paul wrote in his first letter to the Thessalonian Church *"For God has not called us for the purpose of impurity, but in sanctification."* [114] We are called though our election to be set apart from the world; not impure, full of

---

[113] M.G. Easton, *Easton's Bible Dictionary* (Oak Harbor, WA: Logos Research Systems, Inc., 1996).

[114] *New American Standard Bible : 1995 Update* (LaHabra, CA: The Lockman Foundation, 1995), 1 Th 4:7.

sin, but a pure vessel for God to pour out His grace and love. You will notice a difference as you walk this road with the Holy Spirit as your guide. The things that you thought were just an ordinary part of life now become distasteful to you; you cannot abide anyone swearing around you, drunks make you uncomfortable and guys start to actually look at women's eyes. We become increasingly apart from the world's view of normal and see what God considers normal. This is wholly His doing in the Holy Spirit working in you and the Holy Spirit working through God's Word.

When we are in regular study of Scripture we can see more clearly what God expects form us, and how His plan for our future is better that we could even imagine. As become aware of the work that the Holy Spirit is doing in us and through Scripture, we become more "self-aware" of who we truly are. I do not mean that we become self-aware in some new Age, guru driven, contemplate the grass type of awareness, but an awareness of who we are as creatures and who God is as Creator. This leads us to the next simultaneous event: repentance.

Repentance—when God opens our heart to receive Him by the Holy Spirit and to confess Jesus as Savior and Lord, it opens up a new awareness of who we are and how terribly we have lived our lives. We become aware of how holy God is and how unholy we are which leads us to confess our sins and repent. Did you ever notice in some of the science fiction movies when the aliens are attacking, usually New York City, that there is some guy with a sandwich board on a corner with the message "Repent, the end is near." While we may dismiss these people as crazy fanatics, but their message is spot on. The end is near, maybe not for the world, but in our fragile lives we do not inhabit this earth for very long, and we are called to repent before we leave.

To repent means to turn away. That's it, just turn away from sin. Repentance is not self-flagellation as the monks of the Middle-Ages did; it not fasting until you are hospitalized, and it's not removing yourself to some mountaintop to live alone for the rest of your life; repentance is simply turning away from sin. But turning away from sin is not enough, we have to turn TO something. The prophet Isaiah gives us the answer *"Turn to Me and be saved, all the ends of the earth; For I am God, and there is no other."* [115] Repentance is BOTH turning away (from sin) and turning to (God).

Our repentance does not rely entirely on our own power; God works in us to help make us aware of our sins and the need to turn from the. He also gives us the insight to who He is that we can turn to Him. He calls us through

---

[115] *New American Standard Bible : 1995 Update* (LaHabra, CA: The Lockman Foundation, 1995), Is 45:22.

election, regenerates our hearts in re-birth, fills us with His Holy Spirit to guide us in sanctification and the by that same Spirit cause us to reflect on our lives and turn our lives around away from sin and towards a loving God. These are some of the spiritual aspects of our salvation, but there is also a legal aspect to our salvation: justification.

Justification—Consider being in front of the Judge of the universe and having your life judge by what you have done or what you have failed to do. Where is your legal standing? You would be found guilty of violating God's laws, and deserving of punishment. But because of the sacrifice of Jesus God pardons those who have faith in Jesus; we are still guilty, but the punishment for the crime has been fulfilled at the Cross. It would be like you getting a speeding ticket, going before the magistrate, being found guilty, and having the judge pay the fine, only this Judge pays the penalty and declares us righteous.

You may be thinking that this is not fair and that justice is not being served, but a penalty was paid for the sins of believers; the penalty was the death of Jesus on the cross, the perfect blood sacrifice to atone for sins. When we spoke about original sin we said that this sin of Adam was imputed on all generations, well the righteousness of the last Adam (Jesus) was imputed onto those who believe.

> It proceeds on the imputing or crediting to the believer by God himself of the perfect righteousness, active and passive, of his Representative and Surety, Jesus Christ (Rom. 10:3-9). Justification is not the forgiveness of a man without righteousness, but a declaration that he possesses a righteousness which perfectly and for ever satisfies the law, namely, Christ's righteousness. [116]

We are pardoned of ALL sins, past present and future, based on the righteousness of Christ, and the fulfillment of the law. Because of this imputed righteousness there is one more step: adoption.

Adoption—because God has called us, regenerated our hearts, sanctified us by His Holy Spirit, brought us to repentance and justified us through the cross, we are now His children; adopted into His family and made co-heirs of the kingdom with His Son, Jesus. Paul wrote *"For you are all sons of God through faith in Christ Jesus."* [117] and the apostle John wrote *"How great is the love the Father has lavished on us, that we should be called children of God!*

---

[116] M.G. Easton, *Easton's Bible Dictionary* (Oak Harbor, WA: Logos Research Systems, Inc., 1996).

[117] *New American Standard Bible : 1995 Update* (LaHabra, CA: The Lockman Foundation, 1995), Ga 3:26.

And that is what we are!" (NIV)[118] God chose us (election) to be His sons and daughters, not because of anything that we have done or could have done, but because of His grace. This is a new relationship that we have with God; a relationship built on His love for us and by which we can call Him Father.

Conclusion—As you can see, God is active from the beginning, the stirrings in your heart to accept Jesus, to the end, being adopted as sons and daughters into the family of God. His Spirit chips away at the heart of stone to make it into a heart of flesh that is receptive to the Word of God. The causes our re-birth, and guides us on the path of sanctification, and by Christ's sacrifice on the cross, the penalty of our sin has been paid and declared righteous, then God adopts us into His family. This is according to the divine counsel of God; each person of the Triune God is involved in our salvation.

Study Questions:

1. Read Galatians 2:15-21. How does Paul say we are justified?
2. Define election, regeneration, sanctification, justification and adoption.

---

[118] *The Holy Bible: New International Version*, electronic ed. (Grand Rapids, MI: Zondervan, 1996), 1 Jn 3:1.

3. Who is active in each of these?

Meditation Questions:

1. Write out your testimony of how God called you to be His.
2. Is your life reflecting your new birth, consider repentance and the road of sanctification.
3. How does being adopted by God influence your thinking about the love of God?

Part 3

This Life, The Next Life and Beliefs

CHAPTER 7

Death, Heaven and Hell, and the End Times

Death, that fact of life and inevitable end to that life, has occupied man's thoughts since the Fall of Adam. God told Adam that he was going to return to the dust from which he came, and ever since man has, apart from God, tried to explain what happens when we die. The ancient Greeks believed that when a person dies he has to cross the river Styx on a ferry chartered by Charon who had to be paid for the trip. To ensure that the dead made it across the river, they were buried with some coins in their mouth to pay the ferryman. The ancient Egyptians had mummification and magic spells by which the dead would have a secure afterlife, and the Vikings would bury their dead (the common folk) in graves shaped like boats with earthly goods surrounding them. The brave warriors were accompanied into the afterlife by the Valkyries who would search the battlefields for fallen warriors to take them to Valhalla to dine with Odin. So each culture has its own ritual in death and its own belief in the afterlife. As

Christians we rely on God's Word to tell us about what will happen and where we will spend eternity.

The Resurrection—every person will be raised for the dead, both the righteous and unrighteous will be brought up from the grave to face the Final Judgment. There is a misconception out there that only the evil, pagan, unrighteous, non-believer will face judgment, but God tells us that all will be raised to be judged. In Acts 24:15b Paul tells Felix, the governor, *"that there shall certainly be a resurrection of both the righteous and the wicked."*[119] And when we add to that what John wrote in Revelation 20:13b *"and they were judged, every one of them according to their deeds."* [120] we see that we all will stand before the throne of God at the resurrection.

Resurrection is not a concept that is unique to Christianity; the Old Testament is filled with prophecies and descriptions of the resurrection. The prophet Isaiah wrote; *"Your dead will live; Their corpses will rise. You who lie in the dust, awake and shout for joy, For your dew is as the dew of the dawn, And the earth will give birth to the departed spirits."* Not all Jews believed in the resurrection. During the time of Jesus there was a priestly sect of Jews called the

---

[119] *New American Standard Bible : 1995 Update* (LaHabra, CA: The Lockman Foundation, 1995), Ac 24:15.

[120] *New American Standard Bible : 1995 Update* (LaHabra, CA: The Lockman Foundation, 1995), Re 20:13.

Sadducees who denied the resurrection, final judgment and angels. They tried to get Jesus into an argument about the resurrection by asking about a woman whose husband died leaving her childless, and was the custom the brother would then take her as his wife but he too left her childless until all seven brothers married this woman and left her without children. The Sadducees asked "whose wife is she?" Jesus confirms that there will be a resurrection but that marriage in the resurrection will not be. Daniel the prophet in writing about the end of the world wrote; *"Many of those who sleep in the dust of the ground will awake, these to everlasting life, but the others to disgrace and everlasting contempt."*[121] There are many other places within the Old Testament that describes or predicts the resurrection.

In the New Testament we have a clearer picture of both the resurrection and the Day of Judgment. Jesus speaks about this both in parable and in plain words so that His disciples would understand. Jesus' answer to the Sadducees in Matthew 22:29-32 reinforces the idea of the power of God to raise the dead. Much of what we know about the resurrection of the dead comes from the New Testament, and will be discussed in more detail in

---

[121] *New American Standard Bible : 1995 Update* (LaHabra, CA: The Lockman Foundation, 1995), Da 12:2.

the chapter on End Times. For now, let's look at the final resting places after the resurrection.

Heaven—According to Jewish thought, there are three heavens; the first is that area above us in which the birds fly. Psalm 8:8 talks about the "birds of the heavens" or the book of Lamentations speaks of the eagles of the heavens, this is what we can see with a naked eye; the layer of the clouds. The second heaven contain the starry host; that area above the earth that contains all the stars, planets, and moons. Jeremiah writes about "the sun, the moon and to all the host of heaven" in his warning prophecy to Judah. The Old Testament tells us about the heavens that we see, and the Heaven that is the residence of God. Isaiah, in recording God's words to him, wrote "heaven is My throne..." and Solomon spoke during the dedication of the Temple that heaven was God's dwelling place. The idea of heaven is firmly established as God's home, and a place for great blessings.

and My people who are called by My name humble themselves and pray and seek My face and turn from their wicked ways, then I will hear from heaven, will forgive their sin and will heal their land. 2 Chronicles 7:14 [122]

---

[122] *New American Standard Bible : 1995 Update* (LaHabra, CA: The Lockman Foundation, 1995), 2 Ch 7:14.

Heaven in the New Testament—Jesus' teachings about heaven in no way contradict that of the Old Testament ideas, but significantly adds to our understanding of what it is and who is in it. In Jesus's teachings we learn that those who put their faith in Christ will reside with God in heaven. When Jesus was giving His Sermon on the Mount in chapter five of Matthew's Gospel, Jesus tells us that those who are persecuted and insulted because of Him will be rewarded in heaven (Mt 5:11-12). When Jesus sent out the seventy disciples to preach what Jesus gave them, they returned saying that even the demons obeyed because of Jesus' name. But Jesus replied that they should not be happy about that, but they should be happy that their names are written in heaven (Luke 10:17-20). There was no misunderstanding in Jesus' teachings on heaven; in John's Gospel, we hear Jesus calling heaven "My Father's house."

Paul's writings give us another insight to heaven; in his recounting of his vision to the Corinthian Church, Paul wrote that he was taken up into the third heaven, and then a verse later he calls it Paradise. Paul's Hebrew theology is showing through here as discussed above. The third heaven is also called the highest heaven by Solomon in his dedication speech, and heaven of heavens in Psalm 115:16, so Paul's description as the third heaven is in keeping with his Jewish roots. Many his references to heaven are called the "kingdom of God." Although many of his writings about heaven are encouraging, Paul does write about those who will not gain access. In his letter to the Galatian Church, Paul writes:

> *Now the deeds of the flesh are evident, which are: immorality, impurity, sensuality, idolatry, sorcery, enmities, strife, jealousy, outbursts of anger, disputes, dissensions, factions, envying, drunkenness, carousing, and things like these, of which I forewarn you, just as I have forewarned you, that those who practice such things will not inherit the kingdom of God.* Gal 5:19-21 [123]

Paul is pretty clear that those who have not died to the old self, and put on Christ will not be rewarded with heaven. He echoes this in his letter to the Ephesians also, though toned down a bit.

Heaven in Revelation—No single book of the Bible gives a clearer, more exhaustive description of heaven; over forty verses speak about what heaven looks like, the throne that is in heaven, the voices and the angels that come down from heaven and John's trip to heaven:

---

[123] *New American Standard Bible : 1995 Update* (LaHabra, CA: The Lockman Foundation, 1995), Ga 5:19–21.

After these things I looked, and behold, a door standing open in heaven, and the first voice which I had heard, like the sound of a trumpet speaking with me, said, "Come up here, and I will show you what must take place after these things." Immediately I was in the Spirit; and behold, a throne was standing in heaven, and One sitting on the throne. And He who was sitting was like a jasper stone and a sardius in appearance; and there was a rainbow around the throne, like an emerald in appearance. Around the throne were twenty-four thrones; and upon the thrones I saw twenty-four elders sitting, clothed in white garments, and golden crowns on their heads. Out from the throne come flashes of lightning and sounds and peals of thunder. And there were seven lamps of fire burning before the throne, which are the seven Spirits of God; and before the throne there was something like a sea of glass, like crystal; and in the center and around the throne, four living creatures full of eyes in front and behind. (Rev 4:1-7) [124]

---

[124] *New American Standard Bible : 1995 Update* (LaHabra, CA: The Lockman Foundation, 1995), Re 4:1–6.

Much of this description is difficult for us to understand; as much of the book is, but there is a visual that we can relate to; we can see God's throne and we can picture the creatures around the throne, not totally understanding, but visualizing the majesty of heaven.

Hell—Yes its real!

Much of what we know about Hell comes from the New Testament, and wrongly, medieval literature. Jesus teaches quite a bit about the subject, and we need to know the context of His teachings.

Hell in the Old Testament—The place "hell" is not the place that we know as that which those go to eternal punishment, but is more closely resembling the Hebrew place "Sheol" or the Greek "Hades." These are the places of the dead; where people are buried. In the KJV Sheol is translated 31 times as Hell and 31 times as "the grave" and there is really no scholarly consensus as to the true meaning of the word, but most agree that it is the place of the dead. Hades is the Greek equivalent to Sheol. It is the place of the dead before the general resurrection and final judgment.

Sheol is derived from a Hebrew word meaning "to lie waste;"

Sheol then would refer to a desolate, inhuman region where no life can exist and which is a horror to all who behold it. Since such a region was thought to be located under the earth, some have suggested "underworld" as the best translation.[125]

In the prophetic Psalm 16:10, David wrote *For You will not abandon my soul to Sheol; Nor will You allow Your Holy One to undergo decay.* [126] which clearly is meant as grave, the burial place after death as Jesus was not confined to the grave but rose on the third day.

Gehenna—This is the word in Hebrew that best fits our understanding of Hell. Coming from the word *gê hinnōm,* meaning "valley of Hinnom," this was an actual valley south of Jerusalem that was noted for being a sacrificial site where children we sacrifice to Molech during the reigns of Ahaz and Manasseh. During the time of Jeremiah this valley became a burial place for the dead, and began the idea of a place of the damned. Jewish apocryphal (writings that have no confirmed authenticity, are probably not true, and are not part of the canon of Scripture) writing reinforces Gehenna as a place of fiery torment.

---

[125] Allen C. Myers, *The Eerdmans Bible Dictionary* (Grand Rapids, Mich.: Eerdmans, 1987), 478.

[126] *New American Standard Bible : 1995 Update* (LaHabra, CA: The Lockman Foundation, 1995), Ps 16:10.

Hell in the New Testament—The idea of Gehenna is furthered in the New Testament. With one exception, the idea of this place of fire and torment is found only in the Synoptic Gospels in the teachings of Jesus; He calls this place a "fiery abyss" in Mt 9:43, a "furnace of fire" in Mt 13:42 and an "eternal fire which has been prepared for the devil and his angels" in Mt 25:41 Our best image comes from Jesus' parable of the rich man and Lazarus:

> *"Now there was a rich man, and he habitually dressed in purple and fine linen, joyously living in splendor every day. "And a poor man named Lazarus was laid at his gate, covered with sores, and longing to be fed with the crumbs which were falling from the rich man's table; besides, even the dogs were coming and licking his sores. "Now the poor man died and was carried away by the angels to Abraham's bosom; and the rich man also died and was buried. "In Hades he lifted up his eyes, being in torment, and saw Abraham far away and Lazarus in his bosom. "And he cried out and said, 'Father Abraham, have mercy on me, and send Lazarus so that he may dip the tip of his finger in water and cool off my tongue, for I am in agony in this flame.' "But Abraham said, 'Child, remember that during your life*

you received your good things, and likewise Lazarus bad things; but now he is being comforted here, and you are in agony. Lk 16:19-25.[127]

The image that we have of this fiery place of torment is brought about in the book of Revelation; here this place is called the Lake of Fire where John writes that is where those whose names are not written in the Book of Life are found.

Paul does give us a different view of Hell; he never explicitly speaks of Hell as a place of fiery torment, but does address the subject as the just wrath of God. He does not use the concept as a means of getting people to repent, but does use it as a reminder to believers of the fate of those who do not put their faith in Jesus. In Romans 8:12-13, Paul equates belief with life and disbelief with death (Hell).

So Hell is, according to Scripture, a place of eternal punishment (Mt 25:46), a place for the devil and his angels (2 Peter 2:4), where the body will suffer (Mt 5:29), where the soul suffers (Mt 10:28), and as Proverbs 15:24 says, a place where the wise should avoid.

---

[127] *New American Standard Bible : 1995 Update* (LaHabra, CA: The Lockman Foundation, 1995), Lk 16:19–25.

Many ideas about Hell have surfaced in recent and not so recent years. There are some who would claim that Hell is a temporary place and that after a time you just cease to exist; this is in contradiction to Jesus' teaching that Hell is a place of eternal punishments (Mt25:46). Others recently have written that Hell is a temporary "holding place" where you are there for only a short time to pay for your sins and unbelief. These people would say that God could not be that mean to sentence someone to an eternal punishment, but would have them taste what Hell is like. Then on the far side, are those who claim that Hell simply does not exist; that all were redeemed by Christ, and therefore all will go to heaven believer or not. These are not healthy views; they are non-Scriptural, and diminish the justice of God and the power of God. Hell is real, not in the Dante's Inferno type reality, but is a reality where sinners are punished rightly according to God's perfect justice.

The last bit that even among Evangelicals is controversial is the presence of God in Hell. Some would say that Hell is devoid of God's presence; that those who are confined to that place will not see God, nor His glory. If that is the case, where is the punishment? If non-believers are absent from God's presence, they are not losing anything, since they didn't believe in God to begin with, but again, we look to Scripture and see in Psalm 139:8 *If I ascend into heaven, You are there; If I make my bed in hell, behold,*

You are there.(NKJV) [128] Part of the eternal punishment and torment is for all eternity being able to see God's glory but not be part of it. Dr. Tom Ascol wrote:

> To be separated from the Lord and cast into hell does not mean that a person will finally be free of God. That person will remain eternally accountable to Him. He will remain Lord over the person's existence. But in hell, a person will be forever separated from God in His kindness, mercy, grace, and goodness. He will be consigned to deal with Him in His holy wrath.[129]

The End Times

One topic that seems to occupy many minds in the Church is the End Times; also known as "Day of the Lord" in the Old Testament or "Day of Judgment." What occupies the minds are the circumstances of Christ's return, the Millennium, the Rapture, Tribulation, the Apocalypse and what is going to happen here until all things are complete. This whole theology of the end times is called eschatology coming from the Greek word *eschaton* meaning 'last thing.'

---

[128] *The New King James Version* (Nashville: Thomas Nelson, 1982), Ps 139:8.

[129] Ascol, Tom, Dr. The Horrors of Hell, *Tabletalk Magazine*. 2008.

There are many different views of what all these look like and there are churches that make this a fundamental point of their theology. In this section we will look at these ideas using, of course, the Bible as the final word.

Old Testament End Times—During the Old Testament period the Prophets were, for the most part, speaking about the restoration of Israel; the rebuilding of the Temple and Jerusalem, and the re-unification of the Northern and Southern Kingdoms. But, there were a few who did prophesy in regard to what will occur during these last days. Daniel was foremost in his visions of the end times seeing that there would be a war against the saints. In Daniel 7:21-22 he sees that war with the saints winning

> "I kept looking, and that horn was waging war with the saints and overpowering them until the Ancient of Days came and judgment was passed in favor of the saints of the Highest One, and the time arrived when the saints took possession of the kingdom." [130]

Notice that in the end, there is a final judgment with those who remain faithful take possession of the Kingdom of

---

[130] New American Standard Bible : 1995 Update (LaHabra, CA: The Lockman Foundation, 1995), Da 7:21–22.

God. These ideas are echoed by both Jesus and Paul in the New Testament.

End Times in the New Testament—This is where the theology of the end times comes into better view; we have Jesus, Paul and John giving us glimpses into what will happen during those last days, and what it will be like afterwards. First, though, we need to define some terms that are far too often thrown around without a clear understanding of what these terms are.

Tribulation—The Tribulation is that time which Jesus warned about in Matthew 24:21 *For then there will be a great tribulation, such as has not occurred since the beginning of the world until now, nor ever will.*[131] This period will be filled with unprecedented times of trouble, suffering and persecution of the saints. We also get an idea of this from Daniel 12:1 *And there will be a time of distress such as never occurred since there was a nation until that time; and at that time your people, everyone who is found written in the book, will be rescued.* [132] So what they are saying is that during this time we will see things that have never happened before. If we look at Jesus' Olivet Discourse in Mark 13, Jesus predicts wars, famines,

---

[131] *New American Standard Bible : 1995 Update* (LaHabra, CA: The Lockman Foundation, 1995), Mt 24:21.

[132] *New American Standard Bible : 1995 Update* (LaHabra, CA: The Lockman Foundation, 1995), Da 12:1.

plagues and persecutions; it will be a time of suffering for both the saints and the unsaved. Most will agree that this period of tribulation will be relatively short in duration.

Rapture—The Rapture is that event when Christ Himself comes down and takes those who have put their faith in Him to Heaven. In 1 Thessalonians 4:16-17 Paul writes about the Rapture:

> For the Lord Himself will descend from heaven with a shout, with the voice of the archangel and with the trumpet of God, and the dead in Christ will rise first. Then we who are alive and remain will be caught up together with them in the clouds to meet the Lord in the air, and so we shall always be with the Lord. [133]

Where the debate comes is when does Christ return to take His away; does the Rapture come before the Tribulation (1 Thes 4:17), during the Tribulation (Mt 24:15-28) or after the Tribulation (Jer 30:7).

Millennium—Literally, this means a "thousand year reign" and nothing can get a good (or bad) debate going that

---

[133] New American Standard Bible : 1995 Update (LaHabra, CA: The Lockman Foundation, 1995), 1 Th 4:16–17.

taking one of the three major millennial views. Space does not allow me to get into all the sub-categories of these views so we will just concentrate on the three major ones:

Premillennial—In premillennialism, Christ returns before the millennium. The Tribulation has occurred and Christ establishes a millennial kingdom on earth. During this time, the dead will return to life, reunited with their spirits and together with those still alive will reign with Christ for a thousand years. Satan will be bound for a thousand years and will have no influence during this time, and some of the unbelievers who are still alive will come to Jesus and be saved, but not all. Following this thousand year reign, the unbelievers will be raised and there will be the final judgment. The Scriptural basis for this view is Revelation 20:1-10.

Postmillennial—In postmillennialism, Jesus returns after the millennium to judge both the believers and unbelievers. This is a very optimistic view where it is believed that many will turn to Jesus during the millennial period and be saved. Where premillennialism flourishes during periods of persecution of the Church, postmillennialism gains adherents during times of revival in the Church. Postmillennialists turn to Matthew 13:31-33 for the biblical basis for this view. They view the parable of the mustard seed as the growth of the Church before Jesus returns, and the Great Commission of Matthew

28:18-20 as proof that the Gospel will be spread and the Church will grow.

Amillennial—The simplest of the three is Amillennialism. This view of the end times begins with the premise that we are in the millennial stage right now and that there will not be a future millennium. This age of the Church will continue until Christ's return when He will raise both the believers and the unbelievers at which time we all will face judgment.

New Heavens and New Earth—We discussed Heaven earlier but we are told that at the end of times there will be a new earth. God will not destroy His creation and start again, but will renew this earth so that we can continue to live here in our glorified bodies for eternity. According to 2 Peter 3:13, God promises us a new heaven and a new earth in which righteousness dwells, and Paul tells us in Romans 8:19-20 that creation will be set free form decay. What will be different is that we will be in the presence of God in the new creation. John calls this new earth the "new Jerusalem" in which Christ is at the center being the Light for the world. As we look at the description of this New Jerusalem in Revelation 21, it is described as a place of abundant beauty with the gates of pearl and streets of gold (Rev 21:21).

It would be nearly impossible to go into much detail on the subject of the End Times and all the theories surrounding it, and that is not the place for this book, but I did want to give you a very basic understanding of the things you may hear in church and not quite understand.

Study Questions:

1. What is the resurrection and who will be resurrected?
2. How many synonyms can you find for heaven; for hell?
3. Compare and contrast the descriptions in Revelation 4:1-7 and Revelation 21:1-8 with Revelation 20:7-10.
4. Define in your own words Tribulation, Rapture, and Millennium.

Meditation Questions:

1. Read Matthew 25:31-46. Think about your life and your fate; will it be eternal punishment or eternal life?
2. Does the prospect of being absent from God's glory scare you more that the torment of the fire?
3. Why do you think people want to lessen the idea of Hell?
4. Does the differing views on the End Times change the way you live your life in Christ? If so, how?
5. Think what the New Jerusalem would be like as described in Revelation 21. What would it be like to be in the presence of God for eternity?

CHAPTER 8

The Church

The world is driven and tempest tossed by sins. Therefore, God has given to it assemblies— we mean holy churches—in which survive the doctrines of truth. Theolphilus c. 180 AD[134]

The Church; that building on the corner, or that assembly in a rented storefront? What is the Church, how is it (or was it) formed, and what are all those things that the Church does? If you have never been part of a church these are good questions to ask. Some may say that they belong to XYZ Church and that it the right one because their doctrine is the best, or they belong to ABC Church because of some other reason, but what really makes up the Church? Let's look at what the Church is, how it is manifested both locally and universally, and look at what the Church calls sacraments.

---

[134] Bercot, David W. *A Dictionary of Early Christian Beliefs*. Peabody, MA: Hendrickson Publishers, Inc. 2000. 146.

What is The Church?—As always we need to start with a good working definition of what we want to talk about. Wayne Grudem in his book Bible Doctrine defines the Church as "the community of all true believers for all time."[135] In this simple definition there is much to discuss as there are three aspects to this definition:

Community—The New Testament word that is translated as Church is *ekklesia* which means 'assembly.' So a Church is an assembly of people, but what kind of people. In Grudem's definition he says that the Church, the *ekklesia* or assembly is a community. We are all part of some community; one that is defined by similar location, by interests (clubs), or by social similarities. We live in gated communities that are protected from "outsiders" coming in, or we make our communities of interest such that unless you are interested in rock collecting or quilting or surfing, others would not be interested in joining your community. Worst of all are those communities that divide along social/economic similarities. The Church is not/cannot be like this. Paul writes in Gal 3:28 *There is neither Jew nor Greek, there is neither slave nor free man, there is neither male nor female; for you are all one in Christ*

---

[135] Grudem, Wayne. *Bible Doctrine: Essential Teachings of the Christian Faith*. Grand Rapids: Zondervan Publishing House, 1999, 363.

Jesus. [136] The Church does not make distinctions along racial, social or economic lines, but are all one body. Jim Samra wrote in his book, The Gift of Church:

> "while coffeehouse are places where you can find community, church is community. The joining of individual lives, unified by a common experience of salvation, by life of the Holy Spirit, and by a shared sense of mission, is so essential to his design of the local church that God simply refers to the church by this common Greek word, *koinonia*—"the community.""[137]

The oneness of community is reflected in the metaphor of the Church as a body. In Paul's letter to the Ephesian Church and the Colossian Church, we are called the body with Christ as the Head.

All True Believers—The second part of Grudem's definition of the Church is that it is made up of all true believers. Notice in Samra's quote above, that we are unified in our common experience of salvation. All who have confessed Jesus as Lord and Savior belong to the Church. This is

---

[136] *New American Standard Bible : 1995 Update* (LaHabra, CA: The Lockman Foundation, 1995), Ga 3:28.

[137] Samra, Jim. *The Gift of Church.* Grand Rapids: Zondervan Publishing House, 2010, 63.

a major distinction in that there are those who are in the church (sitting in the pews), and those that are the church (the true believers). Not all who fill the pews on Sunday morning are part of the church; they are attending, they may feel good when they are there, but if there is no confession of faith in Christ, they are not a part of the church. Don't get me wrong and think that I am saying that those that are the church are perfect, in fact there is an old joke that says if you find a perfect church, don't join it because if you do it won't be perfect anymore. One of the forbears of the Evangelical Covenant Church said "The doors of the church are wide enough to admit all who believe and narrow enough to exclude those who do not."[138]

For All Time—All who have confessed Jesus as Lord are part of the Church; those who made this confession today and those who confessed under the teaching of Paul two thousand years ago; all are part of the Church Universal and the Church invisible. The Church Universal being all believers regardless of nationality, and the Church Invisible being all believers regardless of time. We may be separated by death, but the Church will come together and be the Bride of Christ on the culmination of this world.

---

[138] Bruckner, James K. ed. *Living Faith: Reflections on Covenant Affirmations*. Chicago: Covenant Publications, 2010, 104.

The Local Church—As opposed to the Church Universal that spans the globe and the Church Invisible that spans time, we are mostly familiar with the local church, the one that you attend every Sunday, the one that maybe you first heard the good news of Jesus in. First we should look at how the local churches are organized, and then how the individual church functions.

Denominations—Unfortunately there are far too many denominations in the Church Universal, but we will concentrate on those denominations that confess Jesus as Lord and hold to the Creeds and Confession of the early Church. For the first millennium there was only one Church, one denomination; this was the Catholic Church, then in 1054 because of a disagreement on the what should be the center of the Church, who should be the head of the Church and other non-salvific issues, the East and the West split into the Roman Catholic Church and the Greek Orthodox Church.

The Church had another major change in 1517 when a Catholic monk named Martin Luther nailed the Ninety-Five Theses on the church door in Wittenburg. This began what is now known as the Protestant Reformation. Among the dividing issues was the power of the pope, the selling of indulgences, and the role of the Church in dispensing grace. Luther was not alone in the reforming of the Church, others like John Calvin, Ulrich Zwingli and others helped form the Protestant Reformation and the ideas that came out of that era. Think of the Church as a tree; at the root is Judaism; we share the idea of the same God, and have thirty-nine books of the Bible in common. Out of Judaism, and the trunk of the tree, is Jesus. The in 1054 A.D. there was what is called the Great Schism; this is when the Roman Church and the Eastern Orthodox churches divided over certain theological and leadership issues. In 1517 A.D. came Martin Luther and the Reformation and several other reformers who led movements to return to a more Bible-centric religion. From Luther we can see a branch that now includes the Lutheran Church. From a reformer by the name of John Calvin came what is known as the Reformed Church. Out of this branch of the Christian tree came the Presbyterian Church, the Baptist Church and the Quakers. From England, and the reformation that was happening in that country come the Anglican Church, the Methodist Church and the Episcopal Church as well as some of the holiness churches. The Roman Catholic has a branch and the Orthodox Churches have a branch, but at the core, the main trunk out of which each of these branches grows is Jesus.

Your Local Church—This is where you are most familiar; the local church where you go to worship and fellowship with other believers. You may meet in a large auditorium type building or a small country church with a white steeple and picket fence around it or you may meet in a school cafeteria until the church is able to build a building, or it may even be in your home. The size of the church does not matter as Jesus says in Matthew 18:20 "For where two or three have gathered together in My name, I am there in their midst." [139]

Being part of the local church means that you now have a community gathered around you in worship, in prayer and in study. The fellowship of the church means that you will not have to walk your walk alone; someone will be there to teach, encourage and if needed admonish you as you mature in Christ; that's what family does. You now have a family of brothers and sisters in Christ; some older and further in their walk with Christ that you to help you, some at your level, and even some that are brand new in their walk with Jesus, but you are not alone.

The local church is where you get the teaching from the pastor in the form of a sermon or from an elder in the church in a small group. The teaching should be orthodox (not some crazy ideas) and should be understandable. If you are not a part of a local church right now, you may be wondering how to find one that is right for you with all the denominations that are out there. First, talk to other believers, and attend their church a couple of times. Make

---

sure that they are preaching and teach biblical principles. If the teacher or preacher never mentions Scripture in his message, odds are that what he is teaching is not biblical but his own ideas; flee from this type of church. Second, remember it's not about you! The measure of a church is not that you go away feeling all happy and glad, but was God glorified in the worship. Was God's presence felt in that church in the music, in the fellowship and in the sermon; that is the type of church that is right. Find a church that has a threefold approach: worship God, nurture believers, and have a focus on evangelism and mercy.

Sacraments—Part of the duties of the local church is to administer the sacraments. A sacrament is defined as:

> A holy ordinance instituted by Christ, in which by sensible signs the grace of God in Christ, and the benefits of the covenant grace, are represented, sealed, and applied to believers, and these, in turn, give expression to their faith and allegiance to God.[140]

In other words, a sacrament is a rite of the church that is a sign and a seal of and for the believer. There are two

---

[140] Berkhof, Louis. *Systematic Theology*, Grand Rapids: William B. Eerdmans Publishing Company, 1996, 617.

sacraments in the Protestant Church and seven in the Catholic Church. We will concentrate on the two that are common; Baptism and the Lord's Supper.

Baptism—Baptism is an outward sign of an inward conversion. It represents the death of your old self and the new life you have in Christ. You can be immersed, poured on or sprinkled, but what is important is that you are willing to make this visible confession to all that you have this new life. This is part of the Great Commission that Jesus gave at the end of Matthew's Gospel; *Go therefore and make disciples of all the nations, baptizing them in the name of the Father and the Son and the Holy Spirit.* [141] Churches differ on the means of baptism, and on who should be baptized; some argue that only confessing believers can be baptized, and others affirm that infants can be baptized. There are good arguments on both sides of this issue, but should not be a dividing point.

The major difference in the theology of baptism lies between the Catholic Church and the Protestant Church. The Catholic view is that baptism is necessary for salvation and the act of being baptized is what causes regeneration (new birth). The Protestant view of baptism is that it is a sign and seal of your conversion; in other words you are

---

[141] *New American Standard Bible : 1995 Update* (LaHabra, CA: The Lockman Foundation, 1995), Mt 28:19.

James W. Ptak

baptized not to be saved, but as an outward sign that you are saved.

The Lord's Supper—This is the sacrament that the Lord Jesus, Himself instituted on the night of His betrayal. Paul recounts this in 1 Corinthians 11

> *For I received from the Lord that which I also delivered to you, that the Lord Jesus in the night in which He was betrayed took bread; and when He had given thanks, He broke it and said, "This is My body, which is for you; do this in remembrance of Me." In the same way He took the cup also after supper, saying, "This cup is the new covenant in My blood; do this, as often as you drink it, in remembrance of Me." For as often as you eat this bread and drink the cup, you proclaim the Lord's death until He comes.* [142]

This is a memorial meal in which Christ is present in the elements of bread and wine (some churches use grape juice). There are three views on the Presence of Christ in the elements. The Catholic view is that the bread and

---

[142] New American Standard Bible: 1995 Update (LaHabra, CA: The Lockman Foundation, 1995), 1 Co 11:23–26.

the wine are transubstantiated, or changed into the actual body and blood of Jesus. The Lutheran view is that Christ is in, with and under the elements, and the third view is that the bread and the wine are symbols of the body and blood of Jesus. These may seem like splitting hairs, but the Church was divided over this issue and one of the reasons why the Lutheran Church and the Reformed Church divided in the sixteenth century.

The Lord's Supper represents His death. The breaking of the bread is the breaking of His body, while the drinking of the cup symbolizes His blood shed for us. Paul writes in 1 Corinthians 11:26 *"For as often as you eat this bread and drink the cup, you proclaim the Lord's death until he comes."* But it is also our participation in His death that is part of this sacrament. We willingly take the bread and the wine, the body and blood of Christ for ourselves, being part of the benefits of Christ's death.

As with Baptism, the Lord's Supper is symbolic in that we are making a conscious, public statement that we are Christ's. We are saying that not only are we His, but He is ours; His death and resurrection we share in. We sit at the table (metaphorically) that He has set, and with this we are seated with fellow believers who also share the hope that is found in Him. Again from 1 Corinthians 10:17, *"Because there is one bread, we who are many are cone body, for we all partake of the one bread."*

Study Questions:

1. What denomination of Church do you attend? Find their "Statement of Belief" or "Affirmations;" do you agree with them? Why or why not?
2. What is the fundamental belief in all Christian Churches? Is this found in the above documents?
3. Have you been baptized; if so what does it mean?
4. Explain the Lord's Supper.

Meditation:

1. The Church is called the Body of Christ. What can make the Church act like a real body?
2. In Baptism, we die to ourselves and are born again in Christ. Coming out of the water represents that new birth. What does to mean to die to yourself?
3. In the Lord's Supper we participate in Jesus' death. What does that mean?

CHAPTER 9

Creeds and Confessions

<u>What are they?</u>—Creeds and Confessions are statements of belief. The word "creed" comes from the Latin word *credo*, which means "I believe." It is a basic statement that can be as simple as one sentence or as in the Apostle's Creed's twelve clearly defined articles. Creeds and confessions are not necessarily man made, but biblical statements with one of the first found in Deuteronomy 6:4 *"The Lord is our God! The Lord is one!"* This is a very basic creed found in the bible, but there are also more advanced creeds in Scripture. Paul in his first letter to the Corinthian Church wrote:

> *For I delivered to you as of first importance what I also received, that Christ died for our sins according to the Scriptures, and that He was buried, and that He was raised on the third day according to the Scriptures, and that He appeared to Cephas, then to the twelve. After that He appeared to more*

than five hundred brethren at one time, most of whom remain until now, but some have fallen asleep; then He appeared to James, then to all the apostles. 1 Cor 15:3-7. [143]

As you can see, this creed declares the death, burial, resurrection and sighting of Jesus after His death in a simple creed that Paul used to teach his readers. Other notable biblical creeds are found in Philippians 2:5-11; Romans 10:9; and 1 John 4:2.

A Confession is a confession of faith; usually a longer more involved statement of faith which is systematically organized. For example the Westminster Confession, which is the Confession of the Reformed Church, has thirty three chapters covering doctrines from God through the End Times and doctrines the explain the Reformed positions on election, predestination and free will. If you want to know what the doctrines of your denomination are, the Confession that they hold to is the place to start. The Westminster Confession of Faith is the document for the Reformed Church and most Presbyterian Churches. The Augsburg Confession is the Lutheran document; there is a Baptist Confession of Faith, a Methodist Confession of Faith and The Savoy Declaration of Faith and Order for

---

[143] *New American Standard Bible: 1995 Update* (LaHabra, CA: The Lockman Foundation, 1995) 1 Cor 15:3-7.

the Congregational Church. Most of the Confessions that we have were products of the seventeenth century as the Protestant Church was developing and denominations were forming.

Why do we need them?—The need for creeds and confessions comes from the fact that we are all sinners and fall short of the glory of God. There have been false teachers and heretics trying to delude and dilute the Church almost from the very beginning. Paul in his letters warns the churches of the false teachers in their midst and to remain in the faith that he taught them. Peter also warns his readers in 2 Peter 2:1 *"But false prophets also arose among the people, just as there will be false teachers among you, who will secretly bring in destructive heresies, even denying the Master who bought them, bringing upon themselves swift destruction."*

The earliest creeds in Scripture were the simple statements of faith, but as the Christian theology developed, there was a need for more formal creeds. In the fourth century there was a heresy led by Arius. It was in reaction to this Arian controversy that led to a council being formed in Nicaea out of which the Nicene Creed was formed. This Arian Controversy, while it accepted the deity of Christ denied His co-eternality with the Father; he held that Jesus was a created being. The debate at this council was what is the essence of Christ, bringing into doubt the doctrine of the Trinity, that Father, Son and Holy Spirit are one in being and one in essence. The council met in 325 AD and formulated the first version of the Nicene Creed, later to be refined in 381AD in Constantinople and finalized in 451 AD at Chalcedon.

The Apostle's Creed—Despite its name, the Apostle's Creed was not formalized by the Apostles. The creed developed over a period of centuries with the variation that we have today finalized in the 10th century. Ambrose, one of the early church fathers, mentions the Apostle's Creed in a letter to Pope Siricius in 390AD. Early forms of the Creed can be found as early as 170 AD with the basic articles of faith, filled out in later forms.

The Nicene Creed—The Nicene Creed came about in reaction to the Araian heresy of the early fourth century. Emporer Constantine called a council of the bishops to work out the differences that were being taught. In 325 AD the council met in Nicea, in modern Turkey and worked out the doctrine of the nature of Jesus; that He is of the same essence as the Father, not a created god. The Council met again in 381 to give us the creed that we have now.

Athanasian Creed—This creed addresses the doctrine of the Trinity in a most complete form in forty-four articles.

Our understanding of the Trinity and the person of Jesus is coalesced in these articles.

Important Creeds of the Church

Apostle's Creed

1. I believe in God, the Father Almighty, the Maker of heaven and earth,
2. And in Jesus Christ, His only Son, our Lord:
3. Who was conceived by the Holy Ghost, born of the virgin Mary,
4. Suffered under Pontius Pilate, was crucified, dead, and buried;
5. He descended into hell. The third day He arose again from the dead;
6. He ascended into heaven, and sitteth on the right hand of God the Father Almighty;
7. From thence he shall come to judge the quick and the dead.
8. I believe in the Holy Ghost
9. The holy catholic church; the communion of saints;
10. The forgiveness of sin;
11. The resurrection of the body;
12. And the life everlasting.

Amen.

The Nicene Creed (c. 381)

We believe in one God, the Father, the Almighty,
maker of heaven and earth, of all that is, seen and unseen.
We believe in one Lord, Jesus Christ, the only Son of God,
eternally begotten of the Father, God from God, Light from Light,
true God from true God, begotten, not made,
of one Being with the Father.
Through him all things were made.
For us and for our salvation he came down from heaven:
by the power of the Holy Spirit
he became incarnate from the Virgin Mary, and was made man.
For our sake he was crucified under Pontius Pilate;
he suffered death and was buried. On the third day he rose again
in accordance with the Scriptures; he ascended into heaven
and is seated at the right hand of the Father.
He will come again in glory to judge the living and the dead,
and his kingdom will have no end.
We believe in the Holy Spirit, the Lord, the giver of life,
who proceeds from the Father and the Son.
With the Father and the Son he is worshiped and glorified.
He has spoken through the Prophets.
We believe in one holy catholic and apostolic Church.

We acknowledge one baptism for the forgiveness of sins.
We look for the resurrection of the dead,
and the life of the world to come. Amen.

Athanasian Creed (c. 500 AD)

1. Whosoever will be saved, before all things it is necessary that he hold the catholic faith;
2. Which faith except every one do keep whole and undefiled, without doubt he shall perish everlastingly.
3. And the catholic faith is this: That we worship one God in Trinity, and Trinity in Unity;
4. Neither confounding the persons nor dividing the substance.
5. For there is one person of the Father, another of the Son, and another of the Holy Spirit.
6. But the Godhead of the Father, of the Son, and of the Holy Spirit is all one, the glory equal, the majesty coeternal.
7. Such as the Father is, such is the Son, and such is the Holy Spirit.
8. The Father uncreated, the Son uncreated, and the Holy Spirit uncreated.
9. The Father incomprehensible, the Son incomprehensible, and the Holy Spirit incomprehensible.

10. The Father eternal, the Son eternal, and the Holy Spirit eternal.

11. And yet they are not three eternals but one eternal.

12. As also there are not three uncreated nor three incomprehensible, but one uncreated and one incomprehensible.

13. So likewise the Father is almighty, the Son almighty, and the Holy Spirit almighty.

14. And yet they are not three almighties, but one almighty.

15. So the Father is God, the Son is God, and the Holy Spirit is God;

16. And yet they are not three Gods, but one God.

17. So likewise the Father is Lord, the Son Lord, and the Holy Spirit Lord;

18. And yet they are not three Lords but one Lord.

19. For like as we are compelled by the Christian verity to acknowledge every Person by himself to be God and Lord;

20. So are we forbidden by the catholic religion to say; There are three Gods or three Lords.

21. The Father is made of none, neither created nor begotten.

22. The Son is of the Father alone; not made nor created, but begotten.

23. The Holy Spirit is of the Father and of the Son; neither made, nor created, nor begotten, but proceeding.

24. So there is one Father, not three Fathers; one Son, not three Sons; one Holy Spirit, not three Holy Spirits.

25. And in this Trinity none is afore or after another; none is greater or less than another.

26. But the whole three persons are coeternal, and coequal.

27. So that in all things, as aforesaid, the Unity in Trinity and the Trinity in Unity is to be worshipped.

28. He therefore that will be saved must thus think of the Trinity.

29. Furthermore it is necessary to everlasting salvation that he also believe rightly the incarnation of our Lord Jesus Christ.

30. For the right faith is that we believe and confess that our Lord Jesus Christ, the Son of God, is God and man.

31. God of the substance of the Father, begotten before the worlds; and man of substance of His mother, born in the world.

32. Perfect God and perfect man, of a reasonable soul and human flesh subsisting.

33. Equal to the Father as touching His Godhead, and inferior to the Father as touching His manhood.

34. Who, although He is God and man, yet He is not two, but one Christ.

35. One, not by conversion of the Godhead into flesh, but by taking of that manhood into God.

36. One altogether, not by confusion of substance, but by unity of person.
37. For as the reasonable soul and flesh is one man, so God and man is one Christ;
38. Who suffered for our salvation, descended into hell, rose again the third day from the dead;
39. He ascended into heaven, He sits on the right hand of the Father, God, Almighty;
40. From thence He shall come to judge the quick and the dead.
41. At whose coming all men shall rise again with their bodies;
42. and shall give account of their own works.
43. And they that have done good shall go into life everlasting and they that have done evil into everlasting fire.
44. This is the catholic faith, which except a man believe faithfully he cannot be saved.

Study Questions:

1. Define what are creeds and confessions.
2. Examine the Confession of your denomination if it has one.
3. What articles of the Athanasian Creed gives the doctrine of the Trinity.

Mediation Questions:

1. How do creeds and confessions affect your walk in Christ?
2. Memorize the Apostle's Creed.

ADDENDUM

Where to Start

After reading this small introduction to Christianity; the Bible and doctrines, we are still left with the question, "Where do I start?" Getting started in anything is the hardest part. Once we get rolling, say for example playing golf or exercising, it gets easier as we progress. But, like golf or exercise, we need to keep it up or else our swing goes bad or our muscles get flabby. Here are a few suggestions to help you get started and to keep on going in your new walk with Christ.

The Church—Getting into a good church is vital for your spiritual growth. We all need to be surrounded by more mature Christians who will encourage us and hold us accountable in our walk. Do not base you church decision on whether there is a rocking house praise band, or the pastor has a dynamic personality. Base your decision on research; ask other Christians where they go to church and if the TEACHING is solid. The best music and most dynamic preacher will not help you grow in the love and knowledge of Jesus, but good, solid preaching and teaching will. Unfortunately there are churches out there that teach that YOU can make yourself better; that YOU can become rich, and that YOU can get yourself into heaven. The reality is that YOU cannot do anything, if you could you would have done it without Jesus, but you can't. So find a good biblical church. Paul wrote in Galatians 1:8 *But even if we, or an angel from heaven, should preach to you a gospel contrary to what we have preached to you, he is to be accursed!* [144]

Small Groups—Get into a small group study. Each church has at least one or two; all women, all men, young adults, teens, singles, or mixed. Find a group that is studying the Bible or some aspect of Christian doctrine and become part of it. You will grow, and in the context of a small group, you will be encouraged in the safety and security of a covenant group.

Bible—GET ONE! Read it daily, cover to cover from beginning to end, or concentrate on one book, but read it; it is God's Word to YOU! There are many Bible reading plans that help you stay on task; chronological, historical, devotional… many types, all with the purpose to give you a plan to read. But, do not read it like a novel; concentrate

---

[144] *New American Standard Bible : 1995 Update* (LaHabra, CA: The Lockman Foundation, 1995), Ga 1:8.

on what God is saying to you at this time. You will be amazed how you will find answers to situations you are in right now that God leads you to. If you want to start with one book, I would recommend the Gospel of John. Start here and then you can move on to the rest of the Bible.

Conclusion

In the preceding pages we have gone through the basics doctrines and beliefs of the Christian faith. Knowledge of these things does not save, only faith in Jesus saves. Once God has called you to be His, then these things are understandable and profitable for your walk and defense of your faith. These are the non-negotiables of the faith; God's Word is true; there is one God in three persons; Father, Son and Holy Spirit. Jesus was born, suffered, died, was buried and rose on the third day for the forgiveness of sins. Christ has set up His body which is the Church where the Sacraments are administered and the Word is preached. Through the years, men have taken God's Word and have twisted it necessitating the formation of creeds and confessions.

To be called by God to be His son or daughter is the beginning of an eternal journey, ending in His presence. As in a marriage, the more you know your spouse, the more you love them; in the same way, the more you get to know your God, the more you will return the love that He has for you. That is why it is important to be in a church, to be in Scripture regularly, be in prayer daily. You are beginning an eternal relationship with your Creator and Savior.

This relationship however comes with a cost; the cost being that things will never be the same, you will grow in the fruit of the Spirit, grow in the love of Jesus, and grow in the love of others. But, your salvation should bear some fruit of its own. We are all to be servants of God and each other. Jesus made it very clear that we are to feed the hungry, heal the sick and visit the prisoner. What that means to you will be revealed as you grow.

May God richly bless your walk with Him, as you grow in the love and knowledge of His Son, Jesus.

To God be the glory!

Suggested Reading

Bloesch, Donald G. *The Struggle of Prayer.* San Francisco: Harper & Row, Publishers, 1980.

Boice, James Montgomery. *Whatever Happened to the Gospel of Grace.* Wheaton, IL: Crossway Books, 2001.

Dockery, David S. ed. *Holman Bible Handbook.* Nashville, TN: Holman Bible Publishers, 1992.

Horton, Michael. *In The Face of God.* Dallas, TX: Word Publishing, 1996.

Morey, Tim. *Embodying Our Faith.* Downers Grove, IL: IVP Books, 2009.

Packer, J.I. *Concise Theology.* Carol Stream, IL: Tyndale House Publishers, Inc., 1993.

Stott, John R.W. *The Cross of Christ.* Downers Grove, IL: IVP Books, 2006.

_. *The Radical Disciple.* Downers Grove, IL: IVP Books, 2010.

Sproul, R.C. *The Holiness of God.* Wheaton, IL: Tyndale House Publishers, Inc., 1985.

_. *The Last Days According to Jesus.* Grand Rapids, MI: Baker Books, 1998.

Wilkinson, Bruce & Boa, Kenneth. *Talk Thru The Bible.* Nashville, TN: Thomas Nelson Publishers, 1983.

Yancey, Philip. *Prayer: Does it Make Any Difference?.* Grand Rapids MI: Zondervan, 2006.

Index